How to Observe Your Group

Fourth Edition

Hedley G. Dimock
and
Raye Kass

Captus Press

How to Observe Your Group, 4th edition

Captus Press Inc.
Units 14 & 15
1600 Steeles Avenue West
Concord, Ontario
Canada L4K 4M2
Phone: (416) 736-5537
Fax: (416) 736-5793
Email: info@captus.com
Internet: http://www.captus.com

Library and Archives Canada Cataloguing in Publication

Dimock, Hedley G., date
    How to observe your group / Hedley Dimock and Rachel Kass. — 4th ed.

(The Group performance & development series)
Includes bibliographical references.
ISBN-13 978-1-55322-137-1

    1. Small groups. 2. Sociometry. 3. Social groups.
I. Kass, Rachel R., date II.. Title. III. Series.

HM133.D56 2007   302.3'4   C2007-900952-2

Canada ▌▘▌ *We acknowledge the financial support of the Government of Canada through the Book Publishing Industry Development Program (BPIDP) for our publishing activities.*

0 9 8 7 6 5 4 3 2 1
Printed in Canada

Contents

Contents

Preface

Writing the preface for this fourth edition is a special pleasure as Raye Kass, my long-time colleague and friend, has joined me as co-author in preparing this edition. Raye brings a wealth of group experience to this series of eight books and particularly this edition. She is the author of her own prestigious book on groups, *Theories of Small Group Development*. Her extensive experience with a variety of community and organizational groups was useful in her work, studies, and reports on the team relationships and training of international astronauts in the United States, Canada, and Russia. The new material in this edition, enlarging it by a third, is chiefly her contribution or inspired by her, including a new theory of group development with its unique focus on learning groups, task groups, and therapy or personal growth groups. Raye has also added a section on the importance of group endings, a topic I have given little attention to in previous editions.

In this edition we have expanded the discussion of the difficulty of observing group conflict as it has such a heavy emotional component. We have tried to point out the value of group disagreements and conflict by making them a more neutral dynamic and encouraging the observations of attempts to manage the conflicts and to not expect resolutions and conflict-free work environments. Also broadened is a comprehensive overview of the ways of looking at group dynamics to give focus to group observations. To emphasize the importance of group theory as the foundation for observation, we have added a unit on adjusting theory for use in observing different kinds of groups.

And, speaking of different kinds of groups, the population mix of Canada continues to change with the thousands of immigrants from all over the world. Toronto is now one of the most multicultural cities in the world, and the racial and ethnic groups that used to be "minority groups" now make up the majority of the population. These population shifts have altered the makeup of many workgroups. As a result, we have adjusted our observation tools to alert readers to these changes in demographics, which may also include seniors with hearing problems;

physically challenged people with special needs; or new Canadians who speak English or French well but may be functionally illiterate when it comes to reading or writing in the workplace language. Cultural norms, values, and expectations of different ethnic groups may also surface as unique dynamics to be observed in your groups.

The shift in readership of this book over the years has illustrated the changing perception in academia and the workplace of the importance of understanding how groups work. These patterns and vicissitudes have varied — from a requirement for professional accreditation, to the requirement that every employee should have two weeks of residential group-work training, to general indifference as other survival, day-to-day needs captured priorities — i.e., recessions, new research on effective treatments, the electronic age, globalization and outsourcing with developing countries, and the jockeying for position of thousands of charities to achieve special status and funding.

The eight books in this series were designed to deal with all the needs and interests of human service workers (health, education, recreation, and community social development and services) throughout their professional careers, and many professions — such as nursing and the applied sciences — have continued to give priority to understanding the factors in working with groups over the years this book has been in print.

In recent years many colleges and universities that use groups in the classroom for projects, case studies, and term papers have adopted *How to Observe* as a text, finding that the quality of learning increased with the effectiveness of the study group. And management educators in several fields have found that classroom project groups experienced all the management principles taught in the book, such as goal setting, leadership, decision making, team building, and conflict management. The students could learn not only the principles from the assigned case studies but from their own real experiences in their groups. Do you think you would learn more from class lectures or from your real experiences in a group?

The new dynamic poking its toe into the operation of human service organizations is the expectation that these publicly and charitably funded organizations will be accountable for assessing the outcomes of their work in terms of their mission and goals (Panel on Accountability and Governance, p. 40). Thus, as universities, for example, start looking beyond the accomplishments of their faculties, class sizes, money spent on student services, and number of books in the library (such as *Maclean's* magazine does in its annual ratings) to what students have learned and how it has enriched their lives and improved Canadian society, we will see an increased interest in understanding the role of groups in education. If and when more outcome planning and evaluation is required to secure public funding, it will have a profound effect on the many human service organizations that use groups as a program method to achieve their mission and goals. A staff that understands how groups work and can facilitate the achievement of its organization's goals will become essential to an organization's future well-being and existence.

As Lewis Carroll said, "If you don't know where you are going, any road will take you there." Effective observation, "the discipline of noticing," is a wonderful skill and is the place to start in increasing your understanding of group process, group behaviour, and group development.

In addition to the joy of working on this edition with Raye Kass and appreciating her solid contribution to it, I'd like to thank Randy Hoffman, CEO of Captus Press. Captus Press took over this series for the human services sixteen years ago and rebuilt it with new editions of all seven books and added an eighth *Outcome-based Program Development and Evaluation*. Randy's keen interest and participation in the format and focus of the series has successfully brought the books into university/college business courses, making us the top selling Canadian books on groups with over 200,000 copies in print. Pauline Lai, this book's manager at Captus Press, is responsible for the new and more readable format, many corrections and additions to the books sources and references, and the beautiful new cover and binding. Working with a new team of authors can also be challenging and Pauline gets our heartfelt appreciation for handling this book's production from conception to print.

Hedley Dimock
Guelph, Ontario

Some Ways of Looking at Group Development

THE ROLE OF THEORY IN GROUP OBSERVATION

"If you don't know where you are going, any road will take you there." — Lewis Carroll

"Whether or not you can observe a thing depends on the theory you use. It is the theory which decides what can be observed." — Albert Einstein

The "discipline of noticing" is a wonderful skill to acquire and develop for it can increase understanding of group process, group behaviour, and group development. But what does this really mean? For some, the "discipline of noticing" might refer to the development of observational skills that focus on the way the group is functioning and/or on how it moves through its various stages. These participants learn to become good "participant-observers," focusing on what is going on in the group while still actively participating within the group. The term *participant-observer* signifies the duality of roles often encouraged in training groups.

For others, *discipline of noticing* might mean focusing on self as a member and learning to become a *witness to one's*

1

own actions. Its active use helps participants develop increased self-insight and self-awareness, often resulting in thoughtful interventions that move the group. This active involvement by a member while simultaneously engaging in observation of self and others makes for responsible membership and effective leadership.

While subscribing to the development of both these skills, this book carries the "discipline of noticing" one step further, namely that of *differentiating observations* instead of engaging in *discriminatory* ones. In so doing this book provides a range of observational tools and theories based on characteristics of effective groups identified by research and theory in the field of group dynamics. Thus, *theory* and not *discriminatory observations* becomes the basis for distinguishing what needs to be observed as it both guides and summarizes research.

This interaction among theory, research, and practice creates a dynamic interdependence. Theory identifies the characteristics of effective groups, research validates or disconfirms them. It is through the practical application of these validated theories in the form of specifically selected "differentiating observations" that existing knowledge is put to use. It is this particular application of this knowledge base that has been central to effective business, industry, and education, and has galvanized the maintenance of group psychological health.

Everyone has their favourite observations when in a group. Some people can tell you what everyone in the group was wearing; others will report how much each person talked; another will notice the bad grammar of any participants; still others will focus on descriptions of the "interesting" people in the group and what they said or did; others will note who seemed to like them or appeared to bond with them. These observations are based on what is of interest to the reporter and what he or she has found important from the experience. The observations represent the predispositions or bias of the reporter and can be described as *discriminating observations*.

Discriminating observations, therefore, tend to be limited to the predispositions, beliefs, and mindset of the observer and are limited in their usefulness in understanding group dynamics. The focus of this book is on *differentiating observations*, based on specific differences identified by group research and theory of group dynamics and development. Kurt Lewin, a founder of the group development movement, used to say that "there is nothing more practical than a good theory" (1951: p. 169) He'd explain that a theory was really a summary of extensive credible research about how something worked. Every good theory about what makes a group tick, therefore, will help identify group dimensions that are important to observe and understand.

The seven theories presented here we have found to be the most useful frameworks to underpin and guide your group observations. They are especially helpful in understanding what you observe, making hunches about what would help the group, and communicating with others about what is happening in the group and would help it move forward. These seven ways of looking at groups provide the focus for the group observation guides included in this book and form the basis for noting the distinguishing characteristics in a group that can lead to understandings and improvements in its success as a group and effectiveness in fulfilling its mission or purpose. These theories provide the road map to get where we want to go and make sure we don't use "any old road" to get there.

All of the theories presented have been used by the co-authors as they have not found that any one theory is best. Rather, they have found that parts of all the frameworks are suitable for different kinds of groups or at different stages of their development. Raye's description of her work with international astronauts and their ground crews (p. 46 of this book) highlights some of the unique operational concerns and group dynamics in play in her role as facilitator/consultant. After you have read over the seven group theories you'll be clearer about what makes the most sense to you for the groups with which you want to use your observation skills. You'll be able to choose several dimensions to focus on for your observations that will help increase your *differentiation specificity*. This contrasts with an experience and personal preference *discrimination* focus.

The overall objective of this book derives from its title, *How to Observe Your Group*, with its intent being the development of a mindful and focused way of observing groups that leads to thoughtful interventions that influence a group's development. The interdependence among research, theory, and practice is underscored throughout this useful and practical book, serving as a tool box that forcefully dramatizes the essentials of group life.

OBSERVING PERSONAL NEEDS

Another book in this series, *Making Workgroups Effective* (Dimock, 1994) emphasizes that all behaviour has some purpose or goal — people don't just do things. If all behaviour of the people you are observing has some purpose, it helps to try having some hunches about what the payoff might be to help focus your observations. A good place to start is with the REAPS model of personal needs, as follows:

Recognition
Experience
Approval
Power
Security

Most frequently in play in groups and organizations are CONTROL and SELF-ADVANCEMENT. *Control* and *power* are attempts to do what you want to do and control the behaviour and activities of other people and the group or organization as a whole. *Self-advancement* refers to the attempt to gain recognition, status, promotion, approval, and material wealth. *Greed* can be a part of self-advancement for when some people find something that works well for them they want more and will end up with diminishing returns and non-functional behaviour. Thus, when you are observing an aggressive dominator, or a dogmatic, reactionary blocker, think *control*. And when you are looking at a posturing egalitarian or a flighty supporter of all opinions, think *recognition and self-advancement*.

The attempts of participants to meet their needs in the group most often show up in the *process* dimension. At any time in the group there is the *content* — what it is that the members are discussing or the activity they are working on — and the *process* — how the group is working and how the members are relating to one another. We call these the "words and the music." The words are the content and the music is the process, and it is the music or process that the sharp-eyed observer is looking at. The extended bickering over when to break for coffee or the minutes of the last meeting are a huge waste of time and make no sense when looked at from a *content* perspective, but the *music* clarifies. They are considered as conflicts over control at the interpersonal, process level. Alfred Hitchcock, the movie director, clarified this idea: "I'm not interested in content, it's the same as a painter not worrying about the apples he's painting, whether they're sweet or sour. Who cares?" (*Time Magazine*, May 12, 1980).

Yes, who cares? It is in the group's process where the important dynamics in the development that determines its success and effectiveness take place. The observation skills described here will increase your influence in the group and help you gain more recognition and status by helping you understand the group's dynamics. And you'll be more effective in making interventions to help move the group forward.

VIEWPOINT I — DEVELOPMENTAL AREAS

The two major contributions of a framework of group development are to identify the areas that are worth observing, and to help explain the relationship among various happenings in the group. The areas of group development identified in this viewpoint are the ones we have used most extensively in our work. They have been regularly updated and were revised again for this edition to reflect their extensive use by nurses, adult educators, community workers, managers, group workers, and college and university students.

Following are the five areas presented in this viewpoint:

• Climate
• Involvement
• Interaction
• Cohesion
• Productivity

These five areas provide a crisp yet comprehensive overview, and while they represent a systems theory of groups, they can be used with the other five developmental models presented here. It has been found that by observing, understanding, and giving attention to these five areas, groups can improve their procedures, accomplish more of their goals, and satisfy more of the participants' needs and interests. (See the Group Observation Guide on page 79 that accompanies this viewpoint.)

Group Climate

Group climate includes both the physical climate or setup and the emotional climate, which can be equally important to the well-being and growth of the group. The physical surroundings should encourage the work of the group — its task accomplishment and the morale of the members. Seating arrangements, lighting, ventilation (smoking), proximity of members, and pleasantness of the surroundings can all affect the group. A gym floor is a poor location for a small group planning session, a theatre-style classroom is a poor choice for a teachers meeting, and rows of benches in a lunchroom do not lend themselves to a board meeting. Moving outdoors to a shady area of grass makes for pleasant surroundings but reduces attention span and interaction possibilities. Tables and chairs increase the orderly decision-making activities of a group, yet an open circle of chairs may result in more personal communication and expression of feeling. Non-verbal communication is quite important in some groups, and if all the members can't see one another, such a group would be handicapped much the same as a group where members couldn't all hear one another.

Perhaps even more important is the emotional climate of the group, which determines the security and acceptance of members. A friendly, informal, accepting climate can encourage trust among members and, by decreasing anxiety, help members to take risks and use their resources. Expectations for the group by the organization (rules and regulations) and the style of the designated leader can also influence group climate.

Group Involvement

Involvement refers to the extent that members are occupied or absorbed with the group. Involvement is usually determined by attraction to the other members in the group and to the mission, activities or product of the group. Involvement may also be encouraged through the overall status and power the group has in the community. Having some stake in the outcome of the group's work also increases involvement.

Following are the key questions in assessing involvement: Why are the members here? What attracts them to the group? What level of commitment do they have to the group? What personal needs are they meeting by belonging? Levels of involvement show up in lateness, absenteeism, and turnover, and inattention and non-commitment to group tasks. Thus the levels of participation and involvement are closely related. Groups with high involvement are most likely to develop a sense of solidarity and cohesion, and become strong, healthy groups.

Involvement can be encouraged by increasing the attractiveness of the group's activities, the satisfactions members receive from interacting with the other members, and the prestige gained through the group's accomplishments. Recognizing members for their unique and specific contributions to the group is one way of gaining this involvement. Opportunities for members to participate in setting their own work goals and procedures are usually very successful in increasing involvement. The use of inter-group competition, awards, and prizes often increases involvement in the short term; yet if they don't relate to the real needs and interests of the members, their effectiveness will quickly wear out.

Group Interaction

Interaction is a key dimension in group development, for the more members interact with one another, the more likely the group will develop and accomplish its tasks. Groups with high rates of interaction tend to be healthier and more productive than groups where there is low interaction or interaction only among sub-groups. Generally, the more people interact with each other, the more likely they are to be attracted to each other and develop solid relationships. Interaction can be encouraged by arranging the physical setup so people can see and talk easily to each other, and by selecting activities that facilitate members' interacting and working together. Group decision-making activities, small group team projects, and coffee breaks promote more interaction than library work or listening to a speech.

Emotional climate is closely related to interaction. Members who feel secure and accepted in a group setting are encouraged to interact with others and to express some of their real feelings, problems, and concerns. Relationship problems, sub-group conflict, and the status hierarchy may get in the way of free interaction. An analysis of the roles of group members described, as Viewpoint II, gives a great deal of information about the interaction of a group.

Group Cohesion

Cohesion, the fourth major dimension of group development, is often called solidarity or unity. It relates to the strengths of the relationships among the members, and can be assessed by determining how well members know and understand each other, and by the degree of feeling they have for the group as their own. In many ways, cohesion is a product of climate, involvement, and interaction. There are groups where cohesion is high, but interaction may not be well distributed or the emotional climate may create insecurity.

Groups with a high degree of solidarity or cohesion are most able to encourage deviant members to accept or compromise with group standards through the group pressure they can exert. Behaviour and attitudes are most likely to be influenced in rather highly cohesive groups that are attractive to the individual members.

A growing group generally becomes more cohesive, although occasionally a group can become too cohesive for its own good, as when members refuse to admit any newcomers and want to work on interpersonal concerns to the detriment of task accomplishment. At this stage of standing still and keeping the same membership, the group may not continue to grow and mature.

A cohesive group pulls together toward common objectives. It is this solidarity that helps the group maintain itself as a group and provides the pressure to encourage members to conform to group standards and work toward common goals. Cohesiveness provides the glue that holds the group together and enables it to achieve its goals.

Group Productivity

The productivity and accomplishments of a group provide much of the motivation for membership and are usually the focus for group interaction. All groups are seen by their members as having goals or tasks to accomplish, and the movement toward these goals influences the satisfaction of the members and the pride in the group as a whole. It is important to study the origin of a group's goals; the integration of individual goals into group goals; the plans or procedures, if any, designed to facilitate the accomplishment of these goals; and the ability of the group to follow the plans and achieve the goals. This involves areas of goal setting, goal clarification in terms of expected outcomes, gaining member commitment, decision making, and implementation.

Styles of leadership within the group and the distribution of member roles play an important part in productivity. As *Making Workgroups Effective* (Dimock & Devine, 1994) suggests, the appropriateness of leadership style in relation to the situational factors of the group is a major influence on group morale and productivity. Therefore, all identified roles in the group — chairperson, advisor, coach, recorder, supervisor, or instructor — should be examined closely to note their impact on the group and their effectiveness.

Relationship Among the Five Dimensions

This approach to group development suggests that there are five major group dimensions that are closely related to one another and that together account for most of the dynamics in any group. As these areas are assessed, analyzed, and understood, and facilitative plans are worked out in a systematic fashion, a group can be helped to grow, increasing the satisfaction of members and the task accomplishments of the group. An observation guide is presented on page 79 of this book that lays out the major points to be assessed under the previous five headings.

VIEWPOINT II — MEMBER ROLES

Leadership may be defined in functional terms as acts that help the group to accomplish its goals or maintain itself as a group. All interactions within a group may be classified as helping the group to accomplish its task, helping the group to maintain itself as a group, or not serving any group function.

The viewpoint of group development from the roles of its members implies that a group needs both task- and group building-oriented participation of members if it is to grow and become fully productive (see Figure 1). All participation can be recorded and classified as one or another of the 14 functions or roles. The observation sheet shown on pages 80–81 has 14 areas in which to classify the verbal interactions of the members. The divisions are as follows:

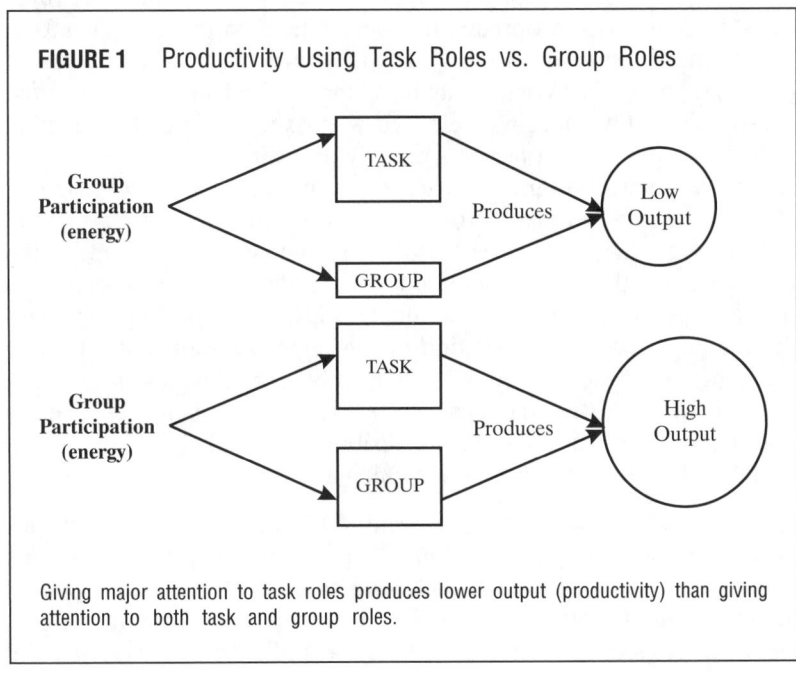

FIGURE 1 Productivity Using Task Roles vs. Group Roles

Giving major attention to task roles produces lower output (productivity) than giving attention to both task and group roles.

Task Roles

1. Defines problems
2. Seeks information
3. Gives information
4. Seeks opinions
5. Gives opinions
6. Tests feasibility

Group-Building and Maintenance Roles

7. Coordinating
8. Mediating-harmonizing
9. Orienting-facilitating
10. Supporting-encouraging
11. Following

Individual Roles (Non-functional)

12. Blocking
13. Out of Field
14. Digressing

Not only does a group need both task and group-building functions, but it needs appropriate functions at the right time. When a football team isn't functioning well, an analysis is made of the different player positions. The centre may be snapping the ball a bit late or the guards may not be blocking their men. All of the roles need to function well if the team is to operate smoothly and win games. In a football squad players are assigned to each position, and they know their job. But a group may have many roles or functions that are not played, and the members may not be aware of these omissions. A review of the roles taken in the group compared to the roles that a group requires (such as the 11 task and group-building roles) points out the gaps. Filling the gaps requires recognition of the importance of these roles or group positions and the ability of the members to take these roles when needed. The ability to take on a wide variety of roles as they are needed in different situations is called role flexibility and is likely to be the most valuable attribute of a fully functioning group member.

The extent to which the 11 essential functions are taken becomes evident through group observation. The performance of these functions may be poorly spread around the group with only two or three people attempting to fill all the positions. This keeps other members from assuming responsibility and is unlikely to utilize the skills of all the

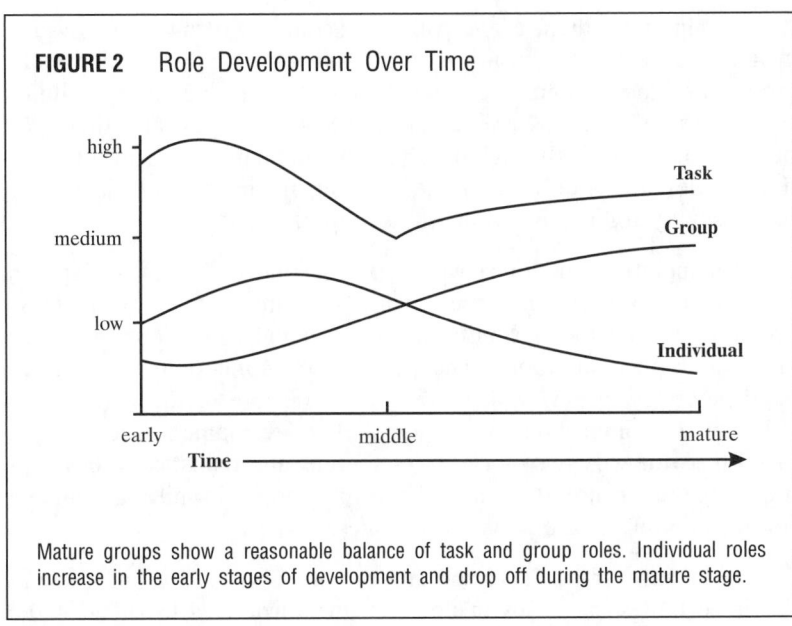

FIGURE 2   Role Development Over Time

Mature groups show a reasonable balance of task and group roles. Individual roles increase in the early stages of development and drop off during the mature stage.

members. Members may not have the opportunity to practise new roles and grow accordingly if two or three people dominate. And if there is domination by a few, the resources of new members are not utilized.

Role flexibility, inadequate role distribution, and missing group functions, once identified through observation and analysis, can be improved by discussion and agreement of group needs and the practice of the needed roles in the group. Individual training through reality practice in out-of-group situations is also helpful.

Groups, during their initial stages of development, tend to be primarily task-oriented. Almost all the participation is at a task level, such as giving opinions and giving information. The development of the group, as well as its productivity, is limited unless it can move into the group-building area.

In fact, the development of a group can be charted by comparing the percentage of task roles to group-building and non-functional roles. The early stages are characterized by a high proportion of task roles with individual roles growing in number. As growth progresses, group roles rise, and individual roles drop off.

In summary, then, a group has to acquire a balance of task and group functions if it is to utilize all its potential as a group. Typically, groups are task-oriented and need help in learning group-building roles. Certain functions are required at specific times, and these can often be determined through observation and analysis. It is also helpful if the roles are widely distributed among members and all assume responsibility for the functions the group requires.

The member-function viewpoint of group development is of special interest to educational and therapeutic programs because of the close relation between the flexibility of an individual's functions in groups and other social situations. The healthy, well-functioning person has been described as one who is able to be flexible in social roles and behaviour. An important part of personality development is learning to take on a wide variety of social roles skilfully and realistically, developing a large repertoire of them, and becoming adroit in shifting from one role to another as the situation changes.

To be sure, the 11 task and group-building roles are but a few of the important social roles in life. Yet an individual's learning of the skills of shifting from one role to another and the ability to assess a situation to know which roles are useful is an important contribution to personal growth. Role flexibility coupled with the effective use of task and group-building roles is an indicator of a flexible, adaptive person who has little susceptibility to behavioural disorders.

VIEWPOINT III — INTERPERSONAL RELATIONS

The following framework for observing, understanding, and talking to others about groups is a continuation of the one started in *Making Workgroups Effective* (Dimock & Devine, 1994), describing the basic needs and development of individuals. The framework is based on the three interpersonal needs proposed by Schutz (1958, 1966, 1989) and has been put into a developmental framework based on our experiences, and those of other writers, about group development. The framework assumes that groups, like individuals, have three basic developmental needs: namely, inclusion, control, and intimacy or openness. The development of a group is handicapped or arrested if each dimension is not resolved in its order of emergence. Thus, a group that has not worked out the inclusion needs of its member in a reasonably satisfactory way is not likely to progress very far into the areas of control and openness. Figure 3 suggests how this works.

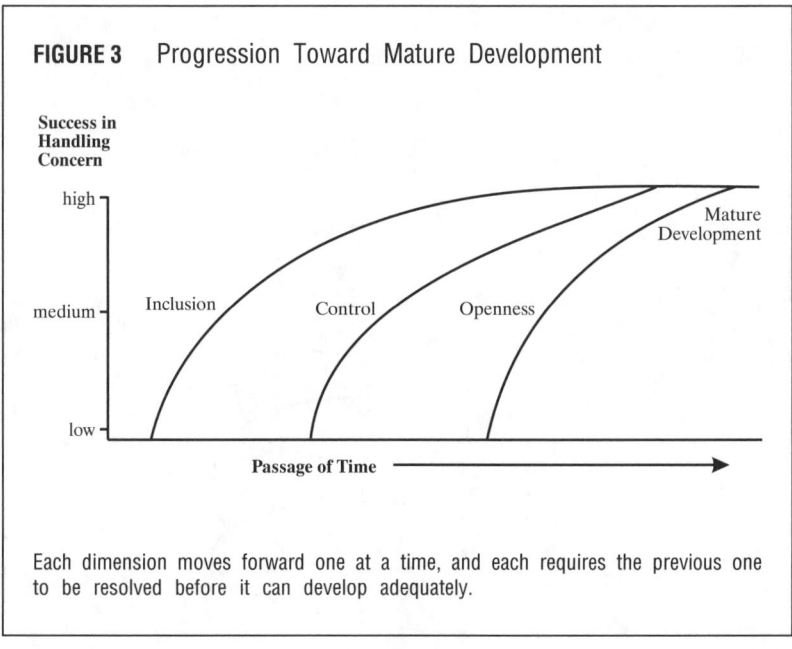

FIGURE 3   Progression Toward Mature Development

Each dimension moves forward one at a time, and each requires the previous one to be resolved before it can develop adequately.

Figure 3 is not meant to imply that a group works on only one factor in growth at a time or always in order. Rather, it suggests a usual order of development, but, once a group is underway, it moves from dimension to dimension as problems come up. In working on and managing these problems, the development of that factor is moved that much further ahead. Over a period of time, the same three issues of inclusion, control, and intimacy continue to surface but at higher or more sophisticated levels. For example, in the early life of a group it may be sufficient for members to ascertain the degree of membership they hold on the group. Later, they may want to experiment with reaching out to bring in a fringe member of the group who has been a cautious participant, or add new members to the group. And later, they may want to test the quality of their acceptance in the group as they take on more authentic roles that are perhaps deviant from the usual traditional roles they first took in order to gain inclusion. We refer to these activities, aimed at achieving a higher level of satisfaction of the three basic needs, as the "helix phenomenon." A helix is an inverted corkscrew, and Figure 4 attempts to show inclusion, control, and openness being dealt with at higher levels of resolution as the group matures.

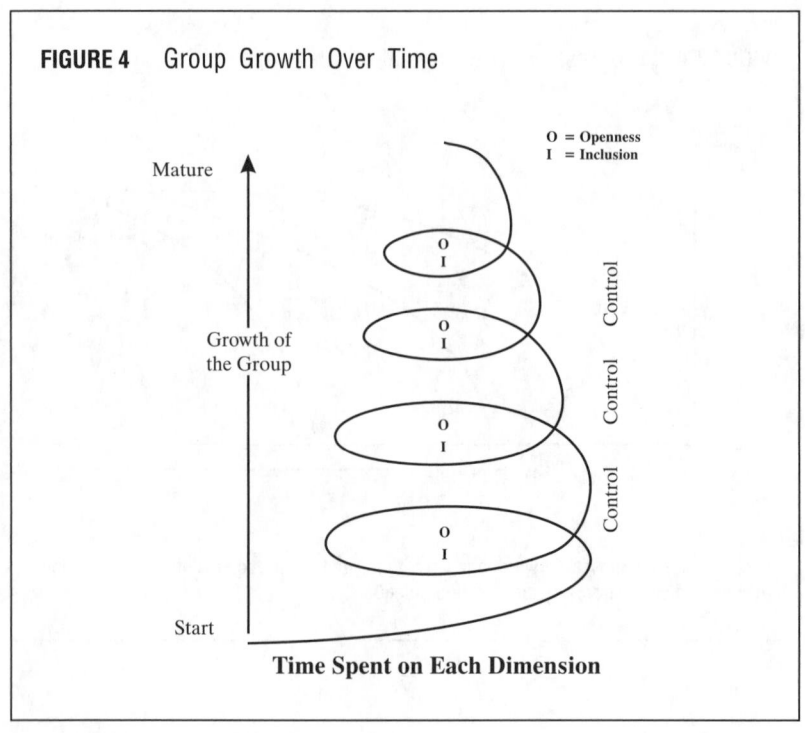

FIGURE 4   Group Growth Over Time

It also shows that as the group starts work, the inclusion of participants takes a fair bit of time — perhaps several meetings. But as the group goes on to resolve the concerns for control and openness and later comes back to improving inclusion, it takes less time. In the mature phase of development the group might work on all three concerns very quickly — perhaps working on all three in one meeting.

As the group moves toward its termination, the helix phenomenon works in reverse. The group leaves its openness phase, moves back to early issues of control, and concludes with a focus of inclusion — namely, disengagement and separation. While the helix highlights the major theme in play, it is rarely to the exclusion of the two other themes.

Most groups start off dealing with these three factors in order. My studies of project groups found that members characterized their early, middle, and late phases with descriptions consistent with inclusion, control, and intimacy. While a middle stage of development may include issues of inclusion and intimacy or openness, most groups describe the predominating theme as one of control.

Schutz (1958) has done some research that suggests groups formed of members who are compatible on these three dimensions will be more effective than other groups. Thus, if a group has some members who want to be in control and others willing to accept that control, it will function better than a group with "all queen bees and no workers." The idea is worth thinking about. While we have not composed groups on that criteria, we have found it useful to look around groups we're working with and ask ourselves (and sometimes the group) how the queen bees and workers balance out.

While it is always difficult and risky to generalize about the growth of a group without knowing its size, physical surroundings, members or goals, the following description creates a framework within which your group can be looked at and compared to other groups. The forms of expression of typical group concerns and the relationships among them may stimulate your thinking about linkages that will make sense in understanding your group. And keep in mind that during all three phases there are the "words and the music" — what the group is talking about or apparently working on and what interpersonal concern the group may really be dealing with at that time. And, while all groups are different, we think you'll be startled to find how well these descriptions fit your group.

Inclusion Stage

During the first few meetings of a new group the members try to get to know each other to see whom they will like and who will accept them. They usually do this by talking about the weather, current events, or perhaps sharing some recent experience (Hedley calls these cocktail issues). This is an effort to establish their *inclusion* in the group and to be recognized and accepted as a member. Part of becoming a member is to know what the group expects of you so you can figure out whether you really want to belong. And it helps for the other group members to know what you expect from the group or why you want to join. As participants balance out what they will need to do and give to gain acceptance, they establish their level of commitment to the group. It is important to assess likely time and financial expectations, usual procedures (will you need to use a computer?), and attitudes and values that the group personifies.

The process of finding out about the group and what it is going to expect, looking over the other participants and making some first impressions of what they are going to be like, and presenting yourself to the group as favourably as you can is difficult and scary. Some participants find this "getting acquainted" process easiest if they jump into the activities or discussion, while others find that sitting back and watching works best for them. This creates a split between over- and under-participators and often becomes an issue in the group as the big talkers try to pressure the quiet members into talking more. While the *words* are about appropriate participation in the group, the *music* is about what participants need to do to become accepted members of this group (who's in/who's out).

Participants may also ask about the goals of the group, the background of the organization to which the group belongs, and the qualifications of the designated leader as a way of sorting out what is going to be expected of them. Some groups try to facilitate this process by having orientation sessions to review goals and procedures, and by telling the participants what is expected of them. Sometimes, too, there is a formal initiation and acceptance ceremony. These structuring activities may help but members still need to work out shared expectations and figure out who in the group likes them and who they are going to like. We have also seen groups, especially those composed of professional human service workers, try to ignore these give/get inclusion concerns and move directly onto specific tasks. This theory assures us that it is not going to work out and that they will soon be back to the unresolved inclusion needs they tried to skip.

As this individually oriented phase moves toward closure, members are usually able to name those who are solidly in the group, those who are halfway in, and who are still on the fringe. Groups that feel inclusion is unresolved may set attendance requirements (miss two meetings in a row and you're out) or other artificial regulations to try and help. At this time, too, members may resist taking in any new members and treat outsiders coolly as ways of protecting the inclusion comfort they have worked so hard to establish. All in all, this phase is a time of hope and trepidation.

Control Stage

The group leaves the inclusion stage with a pretty clear picture of the acceptance level of each member. In the control phase members are trying to work out "who gets to decide what for whom." This means establishing who in the group has what amount of power — i.e., determining the power hierarchy. We call it working out the "pecking order" — the order in which chickens feed. As attention shifts to decision making and to who has influence, there is a fair amount of aggression and conflict as members jockey for position in the control hierarchy.

The relevance of the topics discussed increases during this stage and usually includes how the group will make decisions — majority vote, general agreement, or everyone has to agree. While the *words* do become more important, it is clearly the *music* that is the real focus and that determines successful development. Disillusionment with the group as it bickers leads to discontent — "the group is getting nowhere." Members talk a lot about leaving the group but rarely do.

During the control phase there can be a lot of bickering over very minor points as members attempt to consolidate their positions in the group. Sometimes a member will try to take over the group (which makes the group safe for that person), but the group will not allow it for very long. Another play to make the group safe is to prevent any decision-making procedures from being established and then no one will have to do anything they do not want to do. This can be a more difficult problem to handle, and it may leave the group powerless — an arrested group.

Once the power and influence hierarchy is established and some agreement is reached about how group decision will be made, members relax a bit and start enjoying themselves. Any "pecking order," even if you come in last, is better than none, as ambiguity about position and continuous conflict in pushing for a position is totally unsettling.

Another way to gain control is to establish yourself as a "victim" — someone who deserves special consideration. "I am new to this kind of work..."; "As a single parent with three kids I can't..."; "I don't have the training or experience you all have..."; "I'm not computer literate yet and can't..."; "I am being discriminated against because of my [whatever], therefore..."; and so on. If this kind of a play works, then the person is able to opt out of activities or veto agreements being made without losing position and power in the group. In commercial organizations these perennial "victims" may be pressured to conform to expectations and regulations but can play the discrimination card to maintain their special treatment. Work teams may be able to isolate these people and work around them, but their presence usually affects group morale.

Groups that work through these control issues at an adequate level are able to share the leadership functions among all the members and are consequently able to utilize the full resources in the group. No single member becomes indispensable, and all share in accepting responsibility. As the group increases its solidarity during this phase and sets challenging but attainable goals, it also develops standards for its members that help to facilitate the movement toward agreed-upon goals. As a result, the work level or productivity of the group increases.

With satisfactory solutions to the problems in the control area, there is a great sense of accomplishment in the group. This may create a very high happiness level, where the group feels it is great and attempts to maintain this group harmony past the point of usefulness. As far as the group is concerned, there is no project too challenging, no task too difficult for it to handle. The recognition that this attitude is unrealistic and there are other things to accomplish leads to the next stage of openness and member authenticity.

Openness Stage

The major concern during this stage of group development is working out how open or authentic members are prepared to be with one another considering the purposes of the group. The group starts giving less attention to the status hierarchy and the key players, and more attention to the ideas and unique abilities of each member. There is an acceptance of individual differences and less concern about deviants conforming to group standards as this stage is successfully resolved. The creative members of the group play an increasingly important role and leadership shifts among members in terms of the group task or situation at hand.

As readiness to give and take for the good of the group increases, members volunteer to work with one another in task groups on the basis of who would be helpful in doing the job (rather than the who-likes-whom of the inclusion phase). For example, old Taylor, generally excluded during the inclusion stage because of his reactionary views, is now included for his "historic perspective." Members now see the development of the group in perspective and laugh at the antics of the inclusion and control stages.

Members of the group feel secure with one another and as the trust level develops, there is more sharing of real feelings. This authentic communication and intimacy increases the attraction of the group for members. As personal feelings and opinions are communicated in a direct and open fashion, the data available for problem solving rapidly increases. Efficiency rises as no time is wasted trying to figure out what participants are really saying, or worrying about what strategy is being used on the group. Now each member can be known and treated as an individual, and the unique abilities of each member can be used for the betterment of the group. As the group is no longer hung up on power and control, it may give up "majority rule" and move to group consensus, where all members are committed to action and to taking responsibility for implementation. Resolving conflict is no longer the concern it was during the control stage. The new level of trust and openness can be used creatively for the good of the group.

Termination

As the group moves toward closure, there is an increase of anxiety and unsureness. During their final few work periods many groups regress to immature behaviour that was typical of the early life of the group — power struggles, bickering, and questioning the real commitment of some members. There may be an attempt to downplay the importance of the group and friendships with other members as a way of easing the separation.

In a final attempt to postpone the termination of a group, a reunion or get-together at a later time will be suggested. Most groups realize that this is an artificial effort and, after discussing it, turn it down or just leave it up in the air (the realistic members will say they are too busy and no time when everyone can come will be found). Reunions don't usually happen and, when they do, are an anticlimax — a letdown to the pride and sense of accomplishment of the mature phase of development.

Summary

Groups that have resolved the usual concerns of members in the areas of inclusion, control, and openness are solid, cohesive groups with members who know where they stand in relationship to one another and to the group's tasks. Leadership is typically shared in these mature groups and the designated leader is able to assign and delegate responsibilities with member sanction. While there are clear standards and expectations, the group, because of its solidarity, can tolerate some conflict and the deviant behaviour of its diverse members. A well-developed group is a learning, growing experience for its members, contributing to their self-actualization and physical and mental health.

It is probable that a few groups will not be able to resolve these basic developmental concerns and will either abort or have an arrested development. Sometimes the challenges of getting it all together is just

FIGURE 5   Summary of Viewpoint III — Interpersonal Relations

	Inclusion	Control	Openness
Concern in Play	• Who is in/out?	• Who gets to decide what for whom?	• How do members feel about each other?
Typical Activities	• Minor issue discussions • Creating a good impression	• Jockeying for position • Testing leader	• Interpersonal feedback • Focus on goal achievement
Individual Member Concerns	• What's expected of me? • How much do I want to be a member?	• How much control do I have over myself and others?	• How safe is it to be myself in this group?
Group Growth Concerns	• What is the commitment of each member?	• Settling the "pecking order" and decision-making procedures	• Building authentic behaviour and its acceptance
Dominant Member Feelings	• Insecurity • Excitement • Enthusiasm	• Dissatisfaction • Disillusionment • Competition	• Trust • Acceptance • Goal-orientation
Productivity	• Generally low but high spots on minor procedural issues	• Medium depending on issues used to "jockey for position"	• High if inclusion, control and openness resolved; low if group aborts

too great and the members are not able to mobilize enough to meet the challenge. The group may be too large, have a lopsided sample of prima donnas for members, or a task assignment too tough to handle. The most frequent cause of arrested development is an unresolved control issue. Often it takes the form of one or two rebellious members with low commitment who posture as egalitarian humanists and block all decision making to "protect individual rights."

Human service professionals are candidates for arrested development if they are unwilling to go through the trials and tribulations of group building and imagine that they can establish trust and openness by proclamation, as that is part of their training. Experienced graduate students often have a tough time becoming a group for many of the same reasons. And during the early 1990s and again in the early 2000s with the dot-com bust, the continuous external pressure of the economic recession created havoc in many previously well-functioning workgroups. As their organizations started laying off staff, these groups regressed to immature levels of bickering, hostility and distrust as productivity plummeted.

Hopefully, you have been rather surprised by how much like your group many of these descriptions sounded. Groups are usually rather predictable because of normative processes and self-sustaining goals. An awareness of usual developmental needs and dynamics helps members and designated leaders figure out what is happening in their group and intervene in ways that will encourage further growth and development.

VIEWPOINT IV — WORK AND EMOTION

The work and emotion theory of group development started with the work of Bion at the Tavestock Institute in England (1961) and was given sequential stages for application by associates of the National Training Laboratories in Group Development in the United States (Stock & Thelen, 1958; Bennis, 1964). The theory has been used extensively in classroom groups, human relations training groups, industrial workgroups, and community groups. In order to understand group phenomena, the activities of the group are analyzed in terms of the *level of work* (a little to a lot) and *emotional content*. The *emotional content* is assessed on the continua of fight vs. flight, pairing vs. counter-pairing, dependency vs. counter-dependency, or some combination of these three dimensions.

Flight —Avoidance or denial of the problem, issue or task.

Fight —Hostility and assertion, a direct confrontation of the problem.

Pairing —Expression of intimacy, acceptance, and supportiveness.

Counter-pairing —Rejecting warmth and supportiveness of others.

Dependency —Reliance on a person (leader, teacher, supervisor) or thing external to membership (policies, experts, regulations).

Counter-dependency —Rejection or denial of authority or outside influences.

These categories may be used to describe the group as a whole — e.g., "the group is in a state of flight" — or an individual — e.g., "Dale appears to be very dependent on the designated leader."

Now the work and emotional components of group life are so interrelated that one never occurs without the other. Consequently, the group is always analyzed in terms of its level of work and primary emotional theme (or themes). The emotional quality often determines the level of work and vice versa. A group where members are concerned about their status and are directing *fight* to that concern, probably produces little work. Likewise, a group with an overwhelming task might handle it with emotional *flight*.

At many times a group will not be openly verbalizing an emotional theme such as flight, but the activities of the group can be understood when it is assumed that they are attempting to avoid a problem or task. For example, a group may express interest in a task and apparently be working hard at it, but the more it works, the farther it gets from accomplishing that task. This behaviour can be understood if it is viewed as *flight*, and it can be assumed that underneath the surface the group doesn't want to accomplish the task, or is afraid to try to accomplish it for some reason. Observers must ask themselves, What is this group really trying to do? "It is acting as if it resisted or rejected the designated leader; it is running from conflict of sub-groups," and so forth.

Phases of Group Growth

Groups vary among the emotional themes they appear to be expressing, the level of work, and its relationship to emotionality. When a group is reflective, orderly, and members are listening to one another, it is primarily in a work phase. In response to individual needs or stress it may be disorderly and hostile. At such times, the group is seen as primarily in an emotional phase.

The level of work can range from a low of being unrelated to the objectives and tasks of the group, to a high where there is active problem solving and creative, productive work. The work level of a group usually increases as it continues to meet and emotionality recedes. While there are no exact patterns for groups, the following phases can be expected.

Early Phase

The early phase is characterized by orientations toward authority and, more generally, by the distribution of power in the group. The usual stereotypes that prevail during this phase are that every group needs a strong, competent leader who can move the group toward its goals. It is also believed that certain "necessary" information should be forthcoming (job title, education, family), as each member sees other members as individuals and needs to establish their position in the hierarchy in relation to that member. This phase is characterized by concerns about authority and the usual reaction is one of dependence and flight.

If the structure of the group is seen as vague and unclear, and the designated leader seems weak and ambiguous, a search for goals and objectives — a common group task — results, yet the source of anxiety is the authority figure, not the group's goal. Weak authority figures facilitate the rise of a group member who is assertive and claims to have previous group experience. Dependence on this person works well momentarily, but is doomed to failure. During this phase most behaviour is individually oriented, and the work level is low.

Middle Phase

As the early phase closes there is considerable interaction with the designated leader or authority figure in an attempt to size the person up and determine what rewards and punishments may be forthcoming from various behaviours. It is important to know how much power the designated leader will have so members will know how much control, and in which areas, is left for them to share.

There is more *fight* behaviour among members as they consolidate their positions in the group (this happens in the early phase of children's groups). If the designated leader is directive and encourages dependence, the power struggle among the members is less intense as there is less power up for grabs. But if the authority figure is permissive and unassertive, there will be a more intense power struggle and more counter-dependent behaviour toward the leader. It will take the form of resisting the authority of the designated leader, and playing down the value of her opinions and suggestions. There may even be some discussion about the usefulness and competence of the designated leader, and perhaps suggestions of ways the group could work well on its own.

As the leadership hierarchy becomes more firmly established, there is a lot of pairing and sub-grouping among members. Two sub-groups may compete for power at this stage and, surprisingly, neither may win as power often shifts to the neutral independent group. The *pairing* builds relationships and support, which makes the group more relaxed and enjoyable. The close of this phase may see a honeymoon characterized by "sweetness and light" if the group feels it has worked through its conflicts and disagreements, and feels comfortable with the authority figure.

Mature Phase
The *pairing* and good feelings that members develop during the middle phase increases the attractiveness and cohesion of the group. Group standards evolve, and there is pressure on deviants to conform to these standards. The group becomes more able to maintain itself as a group and operate smoothly within the standards it has set for itself. While the work level during the middle phase is varied, this phase sees a higher level of work and more satisfaction with the work among members.

The destructive conflict and hostility that develops during the middle phase may be managed artificially with a tacit agreement of group harmony. And like real honeymoons, this tends to cover over the expression of any differences or negative feelings. The primary challenge of this mature phase is for the group to work through the compromise and harmony veneer and free up openness and authenticity so it can use the full resources of its members. In recognizing the limitations of the group and the limitations of individual members, a group can build around them.

Maturity is measured by how effectively the group manages tensions, conflicts, and the deviant or creative behaviour of its members. Mature groups collect relevant data on individual and group performance and use it to revise their ways of working — trust, openness, and a readiness to deal with real issues are essential if this feedback is to be used successfully.

The mature phase is one of integration, group flexibility, open expression of individual feelings, the positive use of differing opinions and conflict, and task accomplishment. It is generally characterized as high work and *pairing*, though the group's interdependence is also evident.

In summary, the most noteworthy contribution of this theory is its clarity about the importance of working through the roles and relations with the authority figure in the group. Groups that are unable to get at and deal with this person become stunted in their growth or disintegrate. Designated leaders taking their members through this tricky and unpleasant phase can gain security in understanding that the testing behaviour and hostility has little to do with them personally. Designated leaders whose leadership styles shift from directing to coaching and facilitating in pace with the growth of the group will minimize the trauma of this experience. Effective leadership can also be seen as helping the group through these three phases that have been characterized as (1) *flight* and *dependence*, (2) *fight* and *counter-dependence*, and (3) *pairing* (and interdependence).

VIEWPOINT V — TORI AND TRUST FORMATION

Jack Gibb's TORI theory of personal, group, and organizational development is based on trust — trust in one's self, in other people, and in the organizations and structures they can create. The framework of this theory is based on four dimensions, and TORI is an acronym for these key factors: Trust, Openness, Realization, and Interdependence. But *trust* is the basic component on which the theory is built for it is assumed that without a continuous increase in the trust level in a group, the other three factors will not be able to develop.

Gibb sees fear, a symptom of unresolved trust, as the most crippling feature in personal and group development. People grow as they increase their trust and acceptance of themselves and others. Most non-functional behaviour of individuals and groups can be understood as fear and the facades and defences it creates. Group experiences where members learn how to create trusting, accepting climates encourage individual development and also healthy, productive groups.

In the TORI framework there are four dimensions or modal concerns in group growth:

- *Acceptance* is concerned with the achievement of membership in the group, based on trust.

- *Data flow* is concerned with opening valid, spontaneous communication in the group and translating these data into decision making and choices.

- *Goal formation* has to do with determining member wants and integrating them into problem solving and group action planning, with a goal of productive, creative work.

- *Control* is concerned with leadership, power, and organizational structures that can be developed into freedom-giving, flexible forms.

According to TORI theory, the most revealing aspect of a group's development is a description of the ways in which the early fears in the group are resolved by an increase in trust. Figure 6 on the TORI Group Development Process describes some of the common fears and problems of early group life and what they are replaced with as the group develops more trust in later phases.

TORI is essentially a developmental theory of group growth as there is an optimal sequence in the development of the four dimensions. Yet, the four factors are processed throughout the life of the group and continually flow together and build on each other. Certainly trust and acceptance compose the catalyst for the development of the other three factors if, in fact, they aren't the essential prerequisite. Trusting is an open process, and any high-trust group can't help but be open to highly unpredictable and emergent outcomes. Clearly, this is the most humanistic theory we have presented and, as one of its most important contributions is its openness and flexibility, it would be inappropriate for it to predetermine the usual stages of group growth.

In keeping with this humanistic orientation, the theory also expects the designated leader to be working on the same modal concerns as part of the group. As you noticed in Figure 6, a mature group has integrated the leadership/managing function and does not need someone to

FIGURE 6 TORI Group Development

Modal Concern	Individual Behaviour	Early Development	Later Development
TRUST (acceptance, membership)	• accepting self and others • trusting • expressing warmth • seeing differences	• conformity • fear of adequacy • status seeking • need for role definition	• diversity welcomed • support, encouragement • acceptance of non-conformity • trust and risk taking
OPENNESS (data flow, decision making)	• spontaneity • rapport • depth communication • disclosing	• strategy, caution • ambiguity • secrecy • distortion of date	• clarity, directness • spontaneous expression • listening, sharing • increasing feedback
REALIZATION (goal formation, productivity)	• asserting • exploring • clarifying own needs • achieving	• persuasion, advice • extrinsic motivation • competition, rivalry • apathy, withdrawal	• involvement, creativity • cooperation • common goals • enthusiasm
INTERDEPENDENCE (control, organization)	• participating • cooperating • giving and getting freedom	• dependency • bargain cooperating • giving and getting freedom	• informality • flexible structures • little need for leaders • roles, power irrelevant

Source: Adapted from Gibb, 1978.

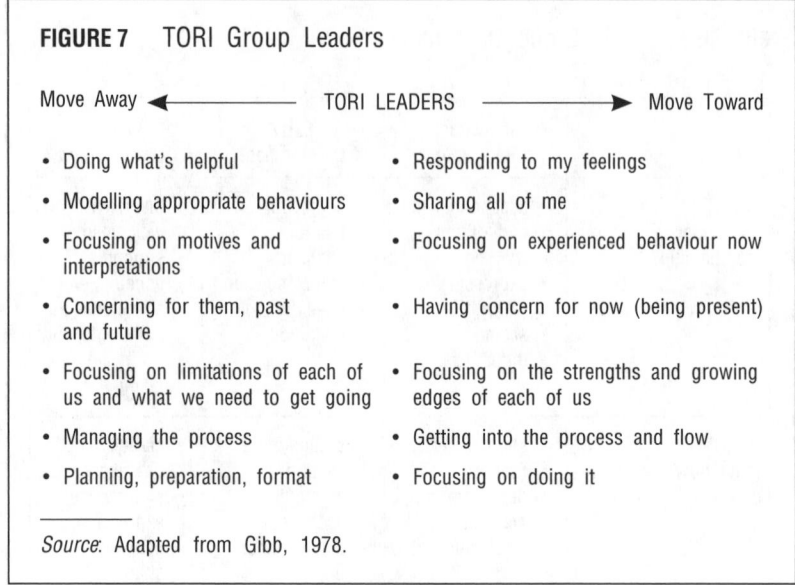

FIGURE 7   TORI Group Leaders

Move Away ◄─────────── TORI LEADERS ───────────► Move Toward

• Doing what's helpful	• Responding to my feelings
• Modelling appropriate behaviours	• Sharing all of me
• Focusing on motives and interpretations	• Focusing on experienced behaviour now
• Concerning for them, past and future	• Having concern for now (being present)
• Focusing on limitations of each of us and what we need to get going	• Focusing on the strengths and growing edges of each of us
• Managing the process	• Getting into the process and flow
• Planning, preparation, format	• Focusing on doing it

Source: Adapted from Gibb, 1978.

organize, teach, manage, or supervise. The basic question for a designated leader using TORI theory is, What would I be doing if I trusted this group more?" Figure 7 gives some suggestions.

VIEWPOINT VI — THE FORMING-STORMING MODEL OF GROUP DEVELOPMENT

Probably the most popular model of group development for group participants is the Forming-Storming approach of Tuckman and Jensen (1977). Certainly the quote we have heard most often from group members we have worked with is "Ah! now we are into the Storming stage of development."

The model suggests that there are four stages of group growth:

Forming — getting started as a group and looking to the designated leader for guidance.

Storming — competition and conflict at the interpersonal level and over goals and procedures.

Norming — acceptance of other members, cooperation, and building cohesion.

Performing — high morale based on pride of task accomplishment and richness of interpersonal relations.

The words speak pretty much for themselves, which may explain why so many people remember the model.

Later, Tuckman added a fifth stage:

Adjourning — movement toward closure: disengagement from relationships and termination of tasks.

The Forming-Storming model uses crisp, colourful words to describe its stages. The original four stages were based on a summary and analysis of 55 group models — about all there were at the time. Ten years later the model was updated on more recent studies, and the fifth stage, adjourning, was added (see Figure 8).

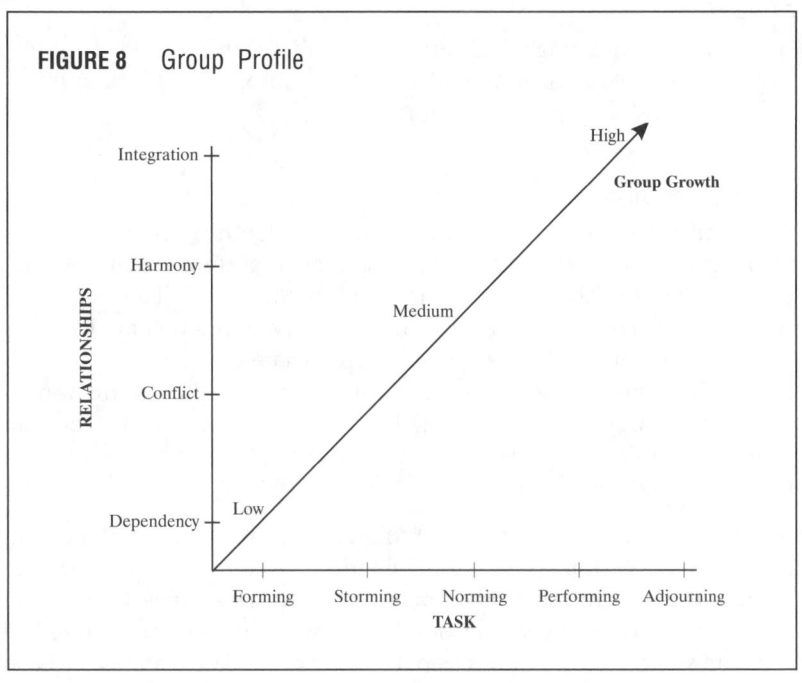

FIGURE 8 Group Profile

VIEWPOINT VII — LACOURSIERE'S LIFE CYCLE IN GROUPS

This is a powerful theory illustrating how a group develops over time. Its usefulness as a theory lies in its practicality and transferability, cutting across a range of contexts and holding true under varied conditions of composition, size, duration, and focus. Students can apply this developmental framework to their task and learning groups; human service and government organizations to their committee and task force teams; and consultants and trainers to their work in the corporate world.

The model represents a five-stage progressive cycle of group development. The stages are ORIENTATION, DISSATISFACTION, RESOLUTION, PRODUCTION, and TERMINATION. They are named according to the predominant theme they represent. These stages occur in a regular sequence, and, while they overlap and blend one into another, they are quite separate and distinct. This does not mean that, once a stage is passed, issues central to that stage do not reappear. Lacoursiere sees few people or groups, as "free of experiences governed by these developmental stages and the associated changes in morale" (Hill & Gruner, 1973).

The following pages will briefly describe each stage, highlighting key dynamics and what to watch out for and observe, and how to translate these observations into actions.

Orientation

While this stage is involved with the usual "getting acquainted" and forming syndrome, the central focus is that of getting oriented to the task at hand. Its focus drives from the term *orientation*. This beginning stage is an interesting one as it is filled with dynamics potentially capable of making or breaking a group. These dynamics are related to what Lacoursiere calls "negative orientation" (when members are forced and/or pressured to participate), heavy reliance on the leader, the setting of unrealistic goals by group members and/or when the task is too vague and unrealistic.

Examples of forced or pressured membership include students who have to take certain prerequisite courses to complete their degree, employees who are required to take on certain task force committees, and members of organizations or educational units who are required to serve on standing committees as part of their mandate. In most groups, however, this stage is striking for its upbeat atmosphere and high morale, with members displaying feelings of optimism, enthusiasm, and expectations that are positive although unrealistic.

> **Observational Tip:** Watch for mandatory participation and unrealistic expectations and statements such as the following:
>
> *"I was asked to join this group. I had little choice in the matter."*
>
> *"I am here because I need this course for my major."*
>
> *"It is great to be here. I am open to whatever needs to get done and certainly don't anticipate any difficulties."*

Dissatisfaction

This is a difficult and frustrating stage, imbued with ambiguity and anxiety. This is also a critical stage because how the dissatisfaction is handled influences commitment, involvement, and resolution in later stages.

Essentially what happens in this stage is the encounter with reality. The unexpected encounter brings into sharp focus discrepancies between expectations and experience. Frustration and anger set in as members begin to realize that things are not what they seemed to be. As these negative feelings prevail, they begin to dominate and far outweigh the more positive feelings experienced in the earlier stage. Environmental influences, member characteristics, nature of the work, prior relationships within the group, negative orientation, and willingness to adapt to the realities of the situation determine the length and depth of this stage. Teams can get bogged down at this stage as morale and work level drops and enthusiasm wanes.

> **Observational Tip:** Watch for unwillingness to adapt to the situation and statements such as the following:
>
> *"Had I known, I would not have volunteered to join this task force."*
>
> *"This is going to take more time than I am willing to give."*
>
> *"I am just going to do the minimal requirement. Nothing more."*

FIGURE 9   How a Group Can Get Stalled in the Dissatisfaction
Stage

While getting stuck is possible in any stage, it is more likely to occur during the dissatisfaction stage, i.e., the unpleasant stage. The list below is derived from Raye's experiences as an academic involved in student and peer groups, and as a consultant involved in training groups in the professional world.

1. When members in the group are unable and unwilling to put aside their differences and focus on the task.

2. When the group refuses to become more realistic about the task at hand, or change to more realistic goals.

3. When the task assigned to the group is vague and impossible to define.

4. When members vary widely in their ability to contribute.

5. When the task assigned to the group is unrealistic and impossible to fulfill within the time frame allotted.

6. When the task assigned to the group is unrealistic because the skills are not adequate to the task to be fulfilled.

7. When a group refuses to acknowledge and own the process it is experiencing — i.e., avoiding to address the inconsistencies that confront the group, and attempting to deny the experienced confusion and vulnerability.

8. When the needs in the group are incompatible with the task needed to be accomplished.

9. When members consistently let down the group by not taking on necessary responsibilities, or by not fulfilling responsibilities they have promised to take on.

10. When difficulties in the group are consistently denied or catastrophized.

Source: Used with permission of Raye Kass from *Theories of Small Group Development*, 3rd Rev'd ed. (Montreal: Centre for Human Relations and Community Studies, Concordia University, 2006).

Resolution

This stage represents closing the gap between expectations and reality. It is here that significant building blocks are laid that influence depth, quality, and success in the production stage. The group begins to challenge the problem, take ownership of its difficulty and examine its goals in terms of time availability. It also starts to test feasibility of proposals checking for practicality and compromising where necessary. Norms that begin to appear are group-oriented, leading to the setting up of structure and procedures that facilitate decision making and task dissemination, thus setting the tone for group cohesion, team-building, and renewed commitment. As morale begins to rise, resources within the team begin to be used. With groups where the dissatisfaction is not deep, this stage is hardly visible, with members moving quickly into the production stage.

> **Observational Tip:** Watch for recognition and ownership of the issue and limitations of the situation and statements such as the following:
>
> *"While this task is not quite what I expected, let us try to make the best of it."*
>
> *"We have wasted enough time bitching and blaming administration. Let us shift our energy into completing our task."*
>
> *"We have sufficient resources among us to accomplish this task. Let us distribute the work and move on."*

Production

It is during this stage that commitment to constructive work begins. Attention is focused on the task with renewed anticipation, high hopes, and positive feelings of eagerness to be part of the experience. Interaction is high, ideas flow, and resources of members become evident. During this stage there is a balance between task and maintenance roles. Time is used both efficiently and effectively with members displaying a willingness to take on responsibilities. This shift in attitude increases productivity with positive morale climbing and reaching a plateau. While enthusiasm and morale are restored in the group it does not mean that the group does not return or *re-experience unrealistic hopes or recurring frustration*. During this high-energy period, morale can drop when the group gets bogged down by overenthusiastic members, overextends itself, is involved in mundane and boring work, experiences the loss of a member, and perceives no end to the task in sight. By and large, however, this is a useful and productive time.

> **Observational Tip:** Watch for validation of member skills, involvement and commitment to the task, and the valuing and appearance of maintenance roles; watch for statements such as the following:
>
> *"Let us regularly stop and check to see how we are doing."*

> *"I had not realized the range of skills in this group."*

> *"I feel committed to this task and am willing to put effort into what needs to get done."*

Termination

This stage is of particular importance in closed-ended groups that have been meeting on a regular basis working toward the completion of a task. The termination stage represents a period of assessment and realistic self-appraisal. Lacoursiere puts forward the thought that while termination signals the ending process of the group, it does not necessarily mean that it comes at the end of the group's development (Anderson, 1985). The *ending process for the group* means that it has reached its end because it has completed its task or because the time allotted has run out, whereas *end of the group's development* signifies that the group has completed its life cycle, having gone through the various stages mentioned previously. This is an important distinction because if termination comes after task completion the group can benefit from this stage, whereas if termination comes before task completion and while in the midst of dissatisfaction, this stage can be, and often is, experienced adversely. Morale can dip or climb depending on the above variables.

> **Observational Tip:** Watch for the level of realistic self-appraisal and/or displacement related to task accomplishment and statements such as the following:

> *"This has been a useful experience. I feel I am leaving having learned a lot."*

> *"While I initially thought this was an impossible task, I feel proud of our accomplishment."*

> *"Had we had more time and had we been given clearer instructions, we would have been able to complete this task. As it stands, we have wasted our time."*

Summary Statement

Lacoursiere's discussion on negative orientation and its ripple effect provide a significant contribution in the area of non-voluntary attendance in groups. In addition, his observation of how a group can get stuck in its development is extremely helpful, since most group development theories do not even make a reference to its possibility, focusing only on the development of the group (Kuypers, Davies & Glaser, 1986). Lacoursiere's discussion on arrestation is constructive in that it draws attention to the possibilities of a group not achieving a complete developmental sequence. It also lends clarity into why many individuals find it difficult to enter new group situations. Further to the above, his presentation of morale as a dynamic, changing characteristic is a useful concept for those who seek intervention guidelines from this model. Lastly, his wide database — e.g., inclusion of more "natural" workgroups he has drawn from to support his ideas for his framework — gives breadth and potency to his model, for it can be applied in both the workplace and in social, therapeutic, and educational settings. (For a more comprehensive treatment of Lacoursiere, see "Lacoursiere's Life Cycle in Groups" [Kass, 2005: Section 1].)

ENDINGS

"Glance ahead and adjust your course accordingly." — Raye Kass

One of the most important and complex stages of a group's development that is consistently overlooked is termination. While much attention has been placed on the development and maintenance of groups, limited research has been done in the area of endings. Here is a focus to help observe this critical stage. (For a more comprehensive treatment of Endings, see "The Hidden Dimensions of Endings" [Kass, 2005: Section 2].)

Endings have to do with closure, an important and often neglected part of the group process. Closure occurs when the purpose of the group has been achieved or when the time allotted for the group has run out. It also signifies a shift in relationships. This is a period of reflection, sharing of learnings and insights and, in some cases, doubts, reservations, and intentions. Morale fluctuates depending on task completion. As in most stages of group development, the process in the termination stage varies according to its focus. However, in all these groups, termination involves coming to terms with both the group's accomplishments and limitations in relation to the task undertaken.

Raye's experience as facilitator/leader/consultant in "one-time" groups (versus ongoing groups) has shown her that unless she has made it part of the agenda, the group does not initiate this termination pro-

FIGURE 10 Versatility of Life Cycle Theory in Groups

A. LEARNING GROUPS

Focus:	Group brought together with the shared goal of fostering learning around a specified area, such as case studies in business, social work or child development, community development, nursing, and organization change.
Membership:	Usually closed. 3–6 persons.
Length of Group Life:	Short term. Approximately 1–10 meetings. Weekly meetings with varying hours.
Leadership:	No assigned leader.

General Developmental Characteristics

Orientation:	Task and socio-emotional areas of behaviour are quite distinct. Initial high enthusiasm. Orientation may be short, particularly if task is clear and skills achievable. If participation is compulsory, there is negative orientation.
Dissatisfaction:	If task is too vague or unrealistic, group can get stuck, with anger directed at authority figures. When members vary widely in their ability to contribute, conflict and unrest appear.
Resolution:	Cohesion, acceptance of differences, and pooling of resources begin to appear.
Production:	Group spends most of the time in this stage. Production is difficult to assess as the processing of learning extends past the group's life.
Termination:	This is influenced by task completion and how long the group has been in existence. Termination may not be an issue if relationships are habitual. If nature of learning is personal, termination may be more difficult.

Continued next page

FIGURE 10 (continued)

B. TASK/WORK-GROUPS & COMMITTEES

Focus:	Group works on a given task with a specific mandate.
Membership:	Closed. Approximately 3–10 persons.
Length of Group Life:	Short term. Approximately 1–10 meetings. Regular meetings with varying hours.
Group Leader:	Usually no assigned leader. May have a chairperson.

General Developmental Characteristics

Orientation:	Task and socio-emotional areas of behaviour are quite distinct. Orientation may be short, particularly if task is clear and mandate specific.
Dissatisfaction:	If task is too vague and unrealistic, group may not move beyond this stage, with anger directed at authority figures. Sometimes the initial stage of high enthusiasm gives way to frustration and disgruntlement when recommendations are not heeded. Unrest and rivalry may appear.
Resolution:	Expectations get adjusted to fit the realities of the task and the restriction of the situation. If task is clear and realistic, this stage is often skipped.
Production:	When task is easy to define and realistic to carry out, group spends more of the time in this stage.
Termination:	This is influenced by task completion and how long the group has been in existence. Termination may not be an issue if relationships are habitual. This stage may last only a few hours.

Continued next page

FIGURE 10 (continued)

C. THERAPY GROUPS

Focus: Personal exploration and understanding of one's motivation, behaviour, and action.

Membership: Open-ended. Usually 5–8 patients.

Length of   Indeterminate. Usually long term, e.g., 1–2 years, 1–2 hours
Group Life: weekly, or more frequently.

Group Leader: Therapist, psychiatrist.

General Developmental Characteristics

In therapy groups, developmental stages are more clearly delineated due to decreased defensiveness and fostering of increased expression of hopes, fears, feelings, etc.

Orientation: Task and socio-emotional areas of behaviour are hard to separate. Task is more difficult to define; thus, orientation lasts a longer percentage of time and blends into subsequent stages. This stage can be even more prolonged because of the open-ended nature of group. Sometimes starts with a honeymoon period, which is short-lived. If participation is involuntary, there is negative orientation with person or group, never reaching the production stage.

Dissatisfaction: Group more commonly gets arrested at this stage. Here, anger is directed toward both leader and group members.

Resolution: Cohesion and the development of group-oriented norms encourage decreased animosity toward leader and increase cooperation among members toward goal achievement.

Production: Since task is hard to define and skills more difficult to acquire, a distinct production stage with a high level of work and positive feelings about it maybe a relatively small part of group life. In excessively long-term groups, production fluctuates because of changes in members' goals or changes in membership.

Termination: Termination becomes part of the task, with feelings of loss examined as part of the process. Since these groups are quite long, there is probably a longer termination stage.

Source: Used with permission of Raye Kass from *Theories of Small Group Development*, 3rd Rev'd ed. (Montreal: Centre for Human Relations and Community Studies, Concordia University, 2006). [Edited.]

cess nor understand its significance until they experience it. What happens with disturbing regularity are apologies, discreetly whispered to her, of prior arrangements to leave early. These announcements are usually peppered with comments, such as "I have to leave earlier but will be here for the most important part" or "please understand it is not that I don't want to be here, but I need to leave before the end" or "that was the only time I could make that appointment" or "in any case I can't be missing much." She is coming to the conclusion that "closure" is a difficult dynamic of life and that most of us have "unfinished business" with endings, transitions, and letting go. Ironically, research has also left this as "unfinished business."

As for groups linked to a larger organizational context, closure occurs in many different ways. Committees often complete their task of assessing their product but not their process. This is a sad commentary because these very same people move on to other groupings with both similar and different colleagues to fulfill new mandates, thus contributing to the functioning of a department or a unit. Obviously, private insights are not verbalized and thus do not get transferred because there has not been a period of assessment and realistic self-appraisal. What is missing is the collective reflection that raises the quality of the system into a learning organization. This means a period of assessment and realistic appraisal of what has been done and what needs to be done. Other types of endings continually occur as colleagues retire, are assigned elsewhere, move on to other interests, or work units, get reorganized, etc.

Termination, whether in "one-time" laboratory or case study groups, or in groups linked to a larger organizational context, plays an important role in the ongoing underpinnings of a system, both on an individual and/or organizational basis. To fail to observe and build in this process is to miss the opportunity to maximize quality, involvement, and task effectiveness.

OBSERVING GROUP CONFLICT

For most people, conflict has about the same appeal as a trip to the dentist. A quick look in a thesaurus offers a clue about its distasteful nature. Synonyms include *battle*, *clash*, *discord*, *hostility*, *strife*, *struggle*, *violence*, etc. We use metaphors to suggest conflict as a kind of a war: "He shot down my arguments"; or as explosive: "Don't blow up!"; or as a kind of trial, in which one party accuses another: "Come on, admit you are guilty"; or even to suggest conflict is a messy business: "Let's not open this can of worms"; or as a dysfunctional force that can be attributed to some regrettable set of circumstances or causes: "They are rivals who always meet head on" or "It's a personality problem."

These words, metaphors, and statements suggest tension, unpleasantness, and vulnerability. They show that we view conflict as something to be avoided. The general assumption in our society is that conflicts are bad and that a good group is one in which there are no conflicts among members. This misconception about the role of conflict in groups creates fear, dread, and mistrust when it does appear and makes it difficult to observe accurately. Being in a high-conflict situation can be upsetting for many people and, thus, may interfere with observation skills. This intervening variable can make it difficult to maintain focus on the group's process — how members attempt to manage the conflict.

Conflict in a group is a neutral dynamic, and the critical issue is how it is managed. Differences of opinion, priorities, values, experiences, and beliefs can be the stimulus for high-quality accomplishments or the group's bane and downfall, depending on how such conflicts are handled. In Canada we see federal elections where the vying parties emphasize the conflict of interests they have with each other and say horrible things about each other. Yet, after the selection of the new head of state, they all get back to work in an organized and usually productive fashion. In other countries the conflicts over who is going to run the country may be determined with bloodshed and the losers jailed or executed. Clearly, the groups' values and methods of resolving the conflict make the difference.

Most social change and scientific discoveries involve disagreements and conflict — the shape of the world, the origin of human beings, the source of diseases, organ transplants, and space travel. History suggests that open and accepting groups of people are more likely than restrictive, totalitarian ones to have these productive, growth-producing activities.

While it is evident from the group theories covered in this book — Schutz, Gibb, and Lacoursiere — that conflict is the most difficult of all phases in a group's development, it is also the most critical, since it provides opportunities for growth, learning and relearning. While conflict creates disequilibrium, it can nonetheless hold the key to enormous learning and growth at both the group and personal level (Kass, 2005). Experience has shown that, while difficult, it is the healthy clash of perspectives and the entertainment of opinions other than our own that brings depth to our work and quality to our decisions, and that motivates our search for creative alternatives and tests and extends our capacities.

In recent years there has been considerable focus on resolving conflicts as though they were a disease that should be cured. Managers were taught *conflict resolution*, and organizations boasted about being conflict free. The approach of this book is that differing opinions and priorities are growth producing, and the focus, therefore, should be on sanctioning them and building their usefulness into the growth of the group. Observation will note what the conflict is about, analyze its source, describe how it is managed, and what seems to help and hinder its usefulness for the group. (For procedures in group problem solving, decision making, and sources of conflict and their management see *Intervention and Empowerment: Helping Organizations Change* [Dimock, 1992] and *Managing Dynamic Groups* [Dimock & Devine, 1996].)

MALE–FEMALE ROLES IN GROUP DEVELOPMENT

A careful observation and analysis over many years of typical roles taken during a group's development show some specific patterns for male and female roles during the various phases. To the extent these patterns play out in your group they add another dimension for observation and understanding. Traditional North American stereotypes are that men will be aggressive, competitive, and dominant, while women will be understanding, warm, and affectionate. And these roles are usually seen as opposites — Venus and Mars — a person has one or the other. Sandra Bem has helped us to look at the roles as two separate dimensions; a person can take on both masculine and feminine traditional roles or behaviour (Bem, 1975; 1977; 1978). Thus, a supervisor may criticize a worker's performance in a tough, assertive manner (stereotyped male roles) yet be sensitive and sympathetic to the disappointment and anger the criticism may create (stereotyped female roles). The blending of the roles usually thought of as masculine and feminine is defined as "androgyny" and the person using both roles as "androgynous." Here are descriptions of the roles and the likely sex of the members.

In the early phase of group development (inclusion or forming), the "male" roles are assertive — those who do most of the talking and focus on the goals and tasks of the group. These people will also suggest rather structured ways to get to know each other. Some of these proposed structures will be followed by the group. In our experience, most of the people taking on these roles will be men. The "female" roles during this stage are not very well heard in the group and, as they are less frequent with low visibility, have little apparent impact. (But people did hear these contributions and refer to them later.)

As the pace picks up during the conflict and storming of the struggles for power and control, the "male" roles become more aggressive. In jockeying for position, two and sometimes three people with strong male roles (usually males but sometimes females) will struggle hard for the top spot. They will line up people to support them, and there becomes two (sometimes three) sub-groups vying for control. A lot of the members — sometimes a majority — will not join either group but will remain neutral during the sub-groups' race for power. Many in this neutral group will have androgynous roles, and there will be more women than men.

The two conflicting sub-groups gradually wear each other out, and the rest of the group grows tired of their bickering and are ready to move on. The catalysts for this move forward are the neutrals, and the emerging leader is a person with both male and female roles.

The androgynous roles of this new leader are most helpful at this stage of development as the pecking order is established and members feel comfortable and secure enough to move on to decision making focused on task accomplishment. The thoughtful and considerate structuring this person does, along with warmth and support for others, are well received. The leadership of this person is well accepted and her status increases. This new androgynous leader is well positioned to help the other members handle the concerns of the openness or mature phase of the group's development. The flexibility of being able to perform both traditional male and female roles coupled with the respite from the aggressive, ambitious and dominating roles of the male leadership style is a winner. This person is self-reliant and independent, and can be forceful and assertive when needed (all traditional male roles), yet she or he is also understanding, sympathetic, and compassionate (traditional female roles). This range of roles with their suitability for the growth needs of the group makes this leader seem very authentic. This builds the trust and openness, the warmth and intimacy required to facilitate the group through the mature phase of its development.

This androgynous leader is usually a woman. In some organizations it is difficult for a woman to be seen and accepted as the leader, and some groups handle this problem by appointing a male as the figurehead leader but using the androgynous woman as the real leader or "power behind the throne." This has often been a satisfactory resolution where everyone was happy (especially if the figurehead male thinks he really is the leader). However, the elevated status and compensation awarded the figurehead, while the actual leadership resides elsewhere, is becoming a sore point in many contemporary organizations. In any case, the leadership roles needed to move a group to full maturity are a combination of traditional male and female roles.

SCAPEGOATING THE ASSISTANT DESIGNATED LEADER

A phenomena somewhat related to this discussion of male–female roles in the group is the attack on the person with whom the designated leader pairs or strongly supports. Hedley's experience is confined to a male-designated leader pairing or supporting a male or female who is seen as the assistant leader. But his female colleagues who are designated leaders in groups and may pair or support a male or female assistant leader tell him the same scapegoating takes place, but with less intensity — especially if they pair with another female.

If Hedley pairs or visibly supports a female member in the group — including the woman who emerges as androgynous leader as described in the preceding paragraph — she will undoubtedly be attacked with many of the feelings of disillusionment and dissatisfaction he has generated for her in pairing with him. She is seen as a substitute for him, and is perceived as being much safer to attack. Anger, disappointment, and hostility are transferred to her, and she is scapegoated for concerns related to him as the authority figure and the source of power. This phenomena also takes place (although not as strongly) if Hedley pairs with or visibly supports a male — perhaps because it seems less safe to attack a male substitute leader than a female; or perhaps there is less jealousy of both male and female members if it is a same-sex pairing (i.e., less perceptions of romantic overtones).

ADJUSTING THEORY USE FOR OBSERVATIONS

CONTROL and STRUCTURE are two dimensions we will compare and contrast at this time to illustrate how theory needs to be adjusted to keep observations focused on the critical issues of the theory. We have reviewed the major role of control in group development in many of the theories. Structure is the new dimension and refers to the clarity and specificity of participants' roles or functions in the group's reason for existence. For example, pro football, baseball, and hockey are all high-structure activities: the players know their positions, what they are to do, and the rules of the game. An overnight hiking or camping trip is less structured: there are no clear rules, and participants do not know what their functions are, which may change with the weather and needs of the group. Nursing in the operating room is highly structured, while nursing in long-term pediatric or psychiatric wards is less structured, as activities change from day to day and patient to patient. Student training groups created to learn about group dynamics and that have an ambiguous purpose are a sharp contrast in structure to a study group in a management course with an outline for an assigned case to report and be graded on.

In high-control groups, the designated leader has the power to make happen whatever is desired. The leader's rule is law and are backed up by punitive authorities, such as failing performance assessments, loss of salary or dismissal. Combining high control with high structure we may think of basic training in the military, operating rooms in hospitals, NASA during a space launching, and the like.

Example One: High Control — High Structure

The early phase of these groups gets off to a smooth start as the power and authority of the leader are clear, the task is definite, and participants know or are told what to do. Concentration on the assigned task at hand follows with little interpersonal activity or immediate concerns about inclusion. Interpersonal interests and needs are worked on informally outside the group.

Example Two: Low Control — Low Structure

In contrast the early stage of these groups opens with the participants trying to find something to talk about to get started. Some security may be found in sharing some interesting but harmless personal information or the "cocktail issues" of the day. These discussions do little to reduce their anxiety about what they are to do and how they are to do it. Attempts to provide leadership in helping the group find common goals or a suitable task usually fail as no one is ready to share control functions until they know how the game will be played and until some trust among participants is developed.

Example Three: High Control — Low Structure

The early phase of these groups tends to be a collection of the vicissitudes of failing groups. The leader is at first accepted and the group appears to get started, but the perceived lack of a purpose, what the group is meant to do and how the group is to do it, quickly labels the leader as incompetent, and everything is up for grabs. If the leader really is incompetent, the group will not develop, it will be stuck and just continue to exist. Possibly, a revolution will take place and the designated leader will be overthrown or immobilized and a new leader will establish the desired purpose and structure for the group. If the leader is competent, there will be a depressing period of disenchantment and an attack on the "assistant leader" may dispel some of the group's hostile feelings toward the leader. As the leader's competence emerges, the group will settle down and start dealing with developmental issues and move forward.

Observational Tips

The activity or "noise" of the groups in these three samples will look entirely different to an observer, yet our theoretical underpinnings make it clear that they are just different ways of dealing with the same early phase of development issues. These are basic personal security issues and the anxiety level (low to high) created by the situation in dealing with them, namely:

- Who gets to decide what and for whom in this group?
- Where, if at all, do I fit into this group?
- Who in the group can I relate to and trust?
- What can I do in this group to gain influence, status, and recognition?

TIP #1: Keep these basic participant needs in mind when watching the action.

TIP #2: Ask yourself what it is members are trying to do for themselves with their verbal statements or lack of them. Think basic needs or what anxiety they are trying to reduce about control or structure.

TIP #3: Watch carefully how members' attempts to meet these needs or reduce their anxiety succeed, if at all.

TIP #4: Also check to see what effect a participant's behaviour has on other individuals or on the group as a whole. Did a pairing attempt succeed, did humour relieve group tension, did a proposal get built upon, did horsing around or playing a victim gain recognition, etc.?

Raye and Hedley usually include some of these kinds of hunches based on these major dimensions of group development theory in their observation notes along with their unbiased behavioural descriptions. This helps them to focus on the process and more appropriately frame any interventions they then choose to make related to their observations.

An Astronaut Example

Raye reports the difficulties she has experienced trying to maintain focus on the group's process while observing high-profile groups under stressful circumstances. In particular she notes her work with international astronauts and cosmonauts in space simulations. The space crew is isolated in a confined capsule for months at a time, where there is no privacy and where video camera and microphone are on twenty-four hours seven days a week. Serious problems that surface can appear as content to be reported and managed rather than as process issues to be observed and understood under the rubric of "ways of looking at groups" underscored in this book.

For example, in a recent Russian space simulation the international crew used English as their language of work, but all communication with mission control directing all the activities of the space crew (telling them what to do, when to do it, and how long they should spend doing it) were entirely in Russian. Thus, the Russian cosmonaut in the international crew who spoke English had special status, particularly as the commander of the international crew could not speak Russian and had to depend on him to translate all messages for him.

Mission control often makes decisions without fully understanding circumstances and dynamics in the capsule, which can increase the crew readiness to resist and rebel, particularly if orders are coming in another language. In fact, on one of the Soviet Salyut space missions it has been reported that there was crew mutiny in which crew cut off all communication with the earth for 24 hours.

These are all common group dynamics related to the "pecking order" gaining status and recognition, control and self-advancement, and inter-dependence and counter-dependence. However, the importance of the mission and Raye's involvement as an observer in such a high-visibility activity (the whole world can hear about it) can easily shift her usual process focus, based on Raye and Hedley's various observation theories, to reporting on the nature and intensity of the tension creating the problem.

You, the readers, may encounter the same challenge to stick to observing the process and want to inadvertently shift your focus to what is upsetting the group when members are getting hostile and sarcastic. This shift in focus from process to content is a common pitfall and remains a continual challenge to those who seriously want to gain the skill and discipline of applying observational frameworks to groups in action to increase knowledge and understanding of the underlying dynamics of what is going on.

"It is the theory which decides what can be observed."
— Albert Einstein

How to Observe
Group Behaviour

2

"You can observe a lot just by watching."
— Yogi Berra

Group leadership is effective to the extent that it facilitates growth of the group and its task accomplishments. To be effective leaders and facilitators, we need to know what is going on in a group and select among our skills and resources accordingly. Direct observation is the most frequently used method to gather information about a group. Sharpening our observation skills, then, is a sure way of making groups more effective. All of us are informal observers of the groups in which we participate, and we informally use our observations in our participation. We observe those areas that have become important to us through our many experiences, and likely pay little attention to other areas. Sharpening our observation skills consists of broadening the variety of areas we observe related to the frameworks of group development, and then making our observations more systematic so that information from one meeting can be compared with similar data from other meetings. As observations are compared over a period of time, ups and downs in the group can be easily spotted and used for group evaluation and long-range planning. If you do not know what is really going on in the group, it is difficult to lead it.

Some kind of an observation guide or set of observation categories helps to make group observations more useful by clarifying which are the important areas or dynamics to watch and by focussing the observer's attention on them. There are so many things to watch in a group that no one could accurately observe half of them, and even if teams of observers watched them all, it would take hours to summarize and process the data. Which areas to select is a judgment based on previous experience but hopefully influenced by a review of suggested observation areas from the literature and the selection of some kind of framework or theory of group development. A guide also helps to make our observations more comprehensive and tends to balance out our tendency to neglect areas not important to us and to have one-sided views. A broadly focussed guide sensitizes the observer to new areas of group interaction, thus checking their usefulness to the observer's frame of reference and intervention strategy.

What, then, is the most useful observation guide — the most important group dimensions to observe? Observation categories should emerge from our views of how groups grow and develop and what the most powerful dynamics are that shape that growth. There are some priority dimensions of group growth that have consistently emerged from group studies and research, and are related to most of the popular group development theories. These are summed up in the Group Observation Guide on page 79. To summarize the essential dimensions even further, focus on procedures for task accomplishment and the resulting productivity; and focus on group-building and -relationship activities, especially those related to power and control.

Observation is the most important method for gathering information about groups because everyone related to the groups is already doing it. With our goal of refining, focussing, broadening, and systematizing observations, it may be beneficial to explore the three major *kinds* of group observers. The first category is the *participant-observer* and includes everyone in the group who is using observations to help figure out what is happening in the group and make their interventions more useful. Everyone in the group is a *participant-observer*, at least unconsciously, but the term is usually reserved for those doing it purposefully.

The second category includes the *designated observer* or assigned group process observer whose goal is to help the whole group understand more about what is happening in the group and motivate members to appropriate action. In the *designated observer* role, the importance of the quality of the data observed decreases, as the reporting skills of the observer more usually determines success. The skill of getting the group to own the observations and do something useful with them is more important than crisp, insightful data that is ignored. Typically, the process observer reports periodically through a group session, or is given a chunk of time at the end of the session. The chief goal of the *designated observer* is to gain acceptance for the data presentation process and stimulate further discussion and analysis of it by the group. This is facilitated by giving descriptive, non-judgmental data on the group and perhaps leaving it a bit open-ended to encourage other perspectives from the group. It is likely that these group feedback skills are harder to learn than those of basic group observation.

The third kind is the *evaluation observer*, who is collecting information for performance appraisal, program evaluation, and planning, or for supervising and coaching the designated leader. If the information is to be used for evaluation, it is particularly important to have standardized observation areas and recording formats to reduce observer bias and increase the comparability of many workgroups, programs, or classrooms.

SO YOU ARE A NEW MEMBER IN A GROUP

How do you quickly look around and get a feeling of what's going on? You want to get accepted fast and not stick out like a country bumpkin new to the city.

Start by getting a first-impression snapshot of the group. Look over the Group Observation Guide shown on page 79 and familiarize yourself with the five observation areas. Don't take it to the group with you and pull it out every few minutes — leave it at home and fill it out when you get back. This will constitute a first-impression snapshot and give you an orientation to the major dynamics of the group. As Yogi Berra says, "You can observe a lot by watching," and, using the Guide to focus your watching, you'll observe more than you can digest for a while.

Each group has its own personality or culture — its usual ways of doing things — that are unique and special to it as a group. The collective behaviour of the members built on the traditions of the group give it this personality. It is important to find out quickly what these "usual ways of doing things" are so you fit in if you choose to do so. These informal rules are not written down anywhere, so they take a bit of "focused watching" to figure out.

The Culture Analysis Observation Guide (Figure 11) will be helpful. Here are some examples of these informal rules to get you thinking about examples from your own experiences:

- Workers arrive at their desks 20–30 minutes before starting time and read the newspaper or a book, have coffee, or make personal phone calls.

- Members can raise and argue any point of view they like but must vote with the chairperson or lose acceptance.

- Workers must wear shirt and tie, blouse and skirt on any day that there is a meeting, and whatever they like (jeans and T-shirt or sweater) other days.

- Everyone liberates office paper, envelopes, pens, clips, etc., for home use, but nobody makes personal use of the photocopier or postage meter.

- To leave your desk and go anywhere (lunch, coffee, washroom) during the day you have to carry a file folder.

- The more clients you carry on paper (you don't need to do anything with them) the higher your status and performance appraisal. Low-status workers compensate by staying late and pushing papers around.

To be sure, some of these informal rules make no sense to the newcomer, yet at some time there was something that started the trend and the rest of the group bought into it and made it part of the culture. Look around carefully, watching the topics highlighted in Figure 11, and don't show a lot of surprise at the unusual things you may find (no one likes to have the illogical aspects of their usual ways of working laughed at).

The other area to be looking at and thinking about is what it is you need to be doing to gain membership and acceptance in this group. An understanding of what the group is going to expect of you as a member and what it is going to offer you are the first questions in play. Then you need to check out the other members and determine who you will pair with — who you like and think may like you. Find out what you will need to do to be a fully accepted member of this group (graduate from the initiation ceremonies and the probation status), and decide whether the gives/gets work out for you. If they do, go for it, knowing you can deviate from the norms and be more of your real self after you have

---

FIGURE 11   Culture Analysis Observation Guide

The goal is to identify the unwritten rules that determine the usual ways in which things work in this community, group, or organization.

- What behaviour or activity gets rewarded? What gets demerits?
- What are the major sources of anxiety and concern?
- What are the norms for dress? Promptness? Attendance? Performance? Deadlines?
- What are the practices for handling routines, lateness, deadlines, absences, and poor performance?
- What are expectations for people to participate in and contribute to the system's well-being?
  - ☐ High
  - ☐ Medium
  - ☐ Low
- What is the amount of support and encouragement given to people here?
  - ☐ High
  - ☐ Medium
  - ☐ Low
- What is the openness/secrecy regarding: income level, competence, performance, promotions or awards, and future professional plans?
- What's talked about privately that isn't addressed publicly?
- How is unacceptable behaviour punished (sarcasm, freezing out, whispering, confrontation, rejection)?
- How are people gotten rid of here?
- How is conflict, aggressive competition, and major disagreement handled?

Source: Adapted from Dimock, 1993.

---

gained full membership and after other members trust you. And, as we have described, if you can avoid aggressive competition for power while you are working out your inclusion, you will have a greater chance to be more influential later on.

In summary, try to move into the group quietly and unobtrusively by getting to know the other members individually as quickly as possible — learn everyone's name fast for you'll never coach a team if you don't know the names of the players. Take a group snapshot, focusing on the procedures for task accomplishment and the group-building, relationship activities — especially those related to power and influence. Then, work on understanding the group's unique culture and unwritten rules for the usual ways of doing things.

Work hard on your own inclusion in the group, and if you decide you want to be fully accepted, let others know your strong commitment to the group and its purposes. And finally, if your early impressions of the group suggest it is operating in a peculiar way that doesn't make much sense, ask yourself what the possible reason or payoff could be for this behaviour:

- A large residential treatment program was constantly facing a crisis, moving from one crisis to the next at about two- to three-month intervals. The director created these crises to give himself directive power and to avoid dealing with everyday people concerns, where he was incompetent. These crises stopped with the coming of a new director.

- An experimental, humanistic school program slowly stopped its programming and spent its time working on the personal problems and relationships of its members. The key players lacked interest and competence in the educational task, and the group's problems became a substitute.

All group behaviour has some purpose, some payoff along the line. Keep looking into the group's history and ascertaining present motivations so that you can continue thinking about what the important norms and dynamics are really all about. This will lead you to working on the improvement of your observational skills.

Improving Observation Skills

We have looked a bit at the basic areas for group observation, and many more observation categories are presented in the pages that follow. The next question is how the observations should be recorded. Before presenting the possibilities and before we start looking at their strengths and weaknesses, let a plea be made to keep your observations simple and straightforward. In Hedley's training programs for group observers, he has them cut in half whatever they had planned to observe before they go into the field as everyone wants to collect much more data than can ever be used. Keep it simple!

In general, observations can be:

1. Put into predetermined categories (roles of group members)

2. Rated (survey of group development, behaviour frequency, observation guide)

3. Tabulated in numerical frequencies (how many times each member spoke)

4. Charted (who spoke to whom, who sat next to whom, who paired with whom for a task)

5. Described in anecdotes (Howard arrived ten minutes late for the meeting and sat down giggling)

6. Recorded in a running account

7. Summarized in a narrative record (see outline in Figure 15 later in this section)

8. Punched into a computer for later systematic analysis

As a participant observer or designated observer, it is important that the observations and their recording doesn't get in the way of reasonably full participation in the group. The observer can prepare for the task by looking over the guide before the session and becoming familiar with its categories or areas. When using the guide for the first few times, it is helpful to have it handy, where it can be referred to during the meeting or perhaps for note taking. After the group session, the observer will take some time to complete recording with the guide.

An observation record will be most useful if it separates objective descriptions from hunches and interpretations. In Hedley's observation records, for example, he puts his subjective observations and hunches in parentheses (members seem to be getting tired of discussing this issue) and his interpretations in brackets [the group seems determined not to let Marilyn take over the group again today]. Usually, he has a lot of questions to himself and the group, and this, too, he separates by putting in parentheses: e.g., (Libby is sure talking a lot — what's got her going?) and (Why has this budget issue come up again — wasn't it resolved in the last meeting?). Another helpful guideline is to review your previous observation records (or those of previous observers) and look for the shifts and changes in the group's dynamics. These shifts are important to monitor as they provide the perspective to fully utilize your group development theory. The impact on the group of various critical incidents can also give more understanding to the shifts and changes.

Designated observers may also be concerned about how they should present their material — guide sheet, recording pages — to the group and how they should describe their role. Opinions vary about how this is best done, but Hedley's strong view is that a straightforward, materials-on-the-table approach is most successful. Observers should briefly describe to the group their interests in observing and the areas they will be watching. When Hedley is the observer, he also mentions who will be reading his notes or how they will be used, and he says that his notes can be read by members anytime. This serves as a convenient introduction to the group of the usefulness of process observations, and may stimulate members to do more thoughtful observing themselves. Members will then be more ready to hear the observer's report, discuss it, and give their own observations about factors helping and hindering the work of the group.

When individuals approach Hedley with questions between sessions, he expresses interest and suggests they bring it up in the group so they can all hear the answers and talk about them. Or he'll get some reporting time in the group and then say that some people have been asking questions and talking about his last observer's report outside the group, and he'll ask what questions they'd like to discuss now that they are together. This helps to get the whole group into the process of discussions and gradually makes it a more accepted use of group time.

If there is to be a training function for the group observer, the ideal situation is for the total group to work out the areas they want to have observed and either take turns being the observer or have a pair of observers do it for several sessions (to get some continuity and comparisons in their observations), and then to pass the task on to a new pair. In Hedley's consulting or program evaluation work with groups, he describes his observation and recording functions and then ask for a volunteer who will join him as an inside observer. This has always worked well in his experience, as the observer who is a regular participant in the group usually has insights that Hedley, as a newcomer, doesn't have. In any case, the more interest and involvement that members have in the observation activity, the more likely that the information generated will be accepted by the group and used in its action planning.

It is important for the observers to find ways of conducting observations without disrupting the group activity or separating themselves from the group. Research on this concern indicates that observing and recording group behaviour and making records does not affect the group's operation if the observer is able to establish rapport with the group. Members and staff usually have this rapport, and new members can build on it by demonstrating real interest in the group's success: tuning in to the group and being open about how the observations will be used by the group and others.

Hedley's concerns are more about how much visibility and attention he, as an observer, wants to have. If he is in a training observer function, trying to motivate the whole group to spend more time and energy on process observation and feedback, he sits centre stage (it's hard to observe if you can't see everyone in the group) and records on 8–1/2 × 11 pages attached to a clipboard or in a loose-leaf notebook. For situations where he wants to minimize the attention paid to his observing/recording function, he either jots occasional notes on 3 × 5 cards or writes in a 4 × 6–1/2 loose-leaf notebook he can slip into his back pocket.

The advent of inexpensive and compact camcorders has increased the use of video recordings as part of the group observation function. Certainly, the cost and size have changed the whole operation since Hedley started using reel-to-reel video, huge cameras, and extra lighting 35 years ago, but most of the same weaknesses and strengths are still there though cost is no longer a drawback. What was received as being the major strength of recording group sessions was that it would provide an unbiased record of the group's proceedings. This hasn't usually been the case, however, as a video camera does not take in the whole of most groups at the same time, and the person controlling the camera must use her biases to decide which part of the action will be recorded (the assertive speaker, the out-of-field pair engaged in side talk, or the enthusiastic supporters in the front row).

The small size of the new camcorders and their ability to record in any amount of light has made them very unobtrusive. And the replay of the group's activity is accepted by all members because the camera does not lie. However, the time involved in getting the equipment operational, then finding segments of the meeting that are useful to replay (few groups can stand watching their whole meeting again), and finally discussing the meaning of the selected segments are rarely more productive for future action planning than a crisp, well-focussed observer's report followed by a high-involvement group discussion. Videos are probably the most useful when providing individuals with objective feedback about their behaviour, and helping the formal group observers check out the accuracy of their recordings. The use of video recordings in assessing personal growth and program evaluation is described in another book in this series, *A Simplified Guide to Program Evaluation* (Dimock, 1987).

One of the most useful contributions of video-recording a group session is in helping the observer improve the quality and accuracy of her records. Watching the video while looking over the observation record of the group's meeting provides the observer with an unusual opportunity to check out perceptions with the very objective record on the tape. If the observer missed any significant incident during the meeting, this will show up in comparing the observation notes to the video recording. Another method of improving observations is to have a team of observers, two or three people, who can compare their notes and pick up on any missed areas. In several of our projects we asked our visitors to take on an observation role with the regular observer and share perceptions. This usually made the session more interesting for the visitor and gave the group the benefit of some fresh insights. Later we set up "observation visitations" with teams of observers from parallel programs attending each other's sessions and reporting on their observations before they left.

The use of video recordings and co-observers is especially useful as a training aide for people just learning observation methods, but video-recordings are also useful in checking and validating information collected through observations. It is always a good practice to try to get three different viewpoints or sources of information to confirm a major conclusion. This triangulation to check accuracy requires that a group observer look for two other sources of information, such as the video recording, a co-observer, informal interviews with the participants, program records of the group, written questionnaires or surveys from the participants, or diaries or records kept by other group members.

In practice, it is usually best to have two independent observers who check their perceptions with the group and follow up by informally interviewing the members after the meeting. If the quality of the information is still in doubt, a three- or four-question Post-Meeting Reaction questionnaire should complete the triangulation and establish beyond reasonable doubt the validity of the information. This kind of validation increases in importance if the information is to be used for comparisons between or among groups or for organization program-evaluation purposes.

Another group observation concern is the balancing of observation areas, such as content and process. *Content* refers to what the group is working on and what it is saying, while *process* looks at how the group is working. This is the analogy to the "words and the music," where the words represent the overt task and concern of the group and the music reflects the real issues or concerns of the members (inclusion, control, intimacy) in working on these tasks.

Over a period of time observers will want to get more "music" into their observations by looking at what people say and do and trying to get at its real intent or meaning, and how it is affecting the group and the person doing it. Often the words of participants, if taken at face value, do not reveal their intended communication: "I think Judi has a good idea here but..." (real meaning, "I disagree"). "I'd like to get some clarification of Gervase's idea, did he mean..." (real meaning, "My opinion is..."). "Let me summarize the ideas presented to date" (one idea is given the spotlight, which seems to be the idea with which the summarizer agrees). Or, if the group continues to flog a dead issue, the observer may feel it is flight behaviour to escape dealing with an intense, interpersonal conflict that has just surfaced. Member interactions should be taken as straightforwardly as possible, but if hunches or interpretations occur to the observer, they should be recorded but clearly identified as hunches or interpretations (parentheses or brackets in the author's records).

In addition to balancing the observations of the content with the process, consideration should be given to balancing observations about individuals with those of the group as a whole. As excitement about an activity or issue increases, there is a tendency to watch the key players very carefully and sometimes miss what the lower-profile participants are doing, what they may be communicating through body language or non-verbal behaviour, or what the overall mood of the group is during the excitement. Checking over an observation guide periodically or setting up time sampling helps to balance observations. And there may even be a moment to note observations of what did *not* happen.

Training Group Observers

As usual, experiential training or "learning by doing" works best for training observers. Basic training can start with making observations and then discussing what was observed with others at the close of the session. More sophisticated training often has observers in training looking over several observation guides, trying out the ones that look interesting in order to gain practice with a broad variety of observation areas, and discussing observations with other observers in training after each practice session. The practice sessions are usually real groups that the trainees are working with, but they may start with simulated group meetings within the training group.

Observers work most effectively and accurately if they design their own observation guide or major areas to observe, and this activity should be facilitated within the training program. In Hedley's training programs, the last activity is for each person to work out an observation plan for observing and reporting on a real group that Hedley brings in for everyone to observe, and then comparing results with the other observers and getting feedback from the demonstration group members.

A lot of group biases and value judgments are likely to appear during early practices. This is quite natural as most people quickly move their descriptive observations to a conclusion or evaluation so they can take action, and it takes considerable practice to record the descriptions first. Observers will report "the room was too smoky" rather than noting that three people asked if the smoking could be limited, and another person opened the window. Or the observer may report that the setting was stimulating and appropriate rather than saying the group met in a library with the walls lined with books and the participants seated around a large rectangular table.

In training sessions, observers pair up and exchange their observation reports. Each person identifies all the conclusions made by the other and asks for the descriptive data that led to making that conclusion. This practice is particularly valuable after an observer finds that, in reporting to a real group, the descriptions are always safe and lead to further discussion, while the conclusions may arouse resentment and close the group off from the observer. While separating descriptions from value judgments sounds fairly easy, it takes most graduate students months to learn, and observer trainees require all of a two-week residential program.

OBSERVATION GUIDES — DEVELOPMENTAL AREAS

Observation guides are something like road maps in that they can save a lot of time and energy and keep people moving into relatively unknown areas from "driving in circles." Even very experienced drivers will consult a road map to figure out the most desirable route to their destination. Some will take the shortest route and conserve on energy consumption, others will take the fastest route, figuring that time is money, and some prefer the scenic route and try to avoid major congested areas. In any case, after travelling the areas many times the road map may be checked periodically to make sure something isn't being missed, but the map is usually put away. The following selection of guides and observation tools are useful in exploring relatively new territory and checking from time to time that there aren't available perhaps tougher but more productive pathways to group development. In the long run, such guides and tools should be set aside as observers develop their own guides based on the specific needs and problems of the groups with whom they are working and as they develop their own theories of group development.

Group Observation Guide

Following the sequence of viewpoints of group development presented in the last section, the first guide is set up to remind the observer of the points to look for under the five major areas of a group's operation. This guide is designed be placed in front of the observer, preferably stapled to a file folder and opened like a book, which makes it a bit easier to handle. Look at the guide on page 79 and you will notice a number of different sub-questions phrased in just a few words, leaving very little space for an extended answer. It is expected that the observer will glance over the guide sheet every so often during a meeting or activity and make a note or two of something that has become clear. Very little is written during the activity, but the constant thinking about these areas plus the few notes enable the observer to complete the record or write it up in a narrative fashion after the meeting. After the observer is familiar with the categories, he or she can participate with the group in the normal way and not be tied down to making more than a few notes with the guide sheet. Watching and participating in the group comes first, making notes second.

Many of the questions raised in all five sections of this guide are appropriate ones to ask the group members or to raise for discussion: "To what extent are the problems we worked on today important ones to you?" "Why?" "To what extent did you all understand our goal, what we were trying to accomplish?" "What pressure, if any, did you feel to change your opinion and go along with the majority?" If this can be done, it helps the observer check the observations.

Under the heading "Interaction" it is suggested that who speaks to whom is worth noting. Do the members usually talk to one or two people (the designated leader or the power figures), to a best friend, or to everyone? An additional page can be added for the interaction diagram and additional comments on roles of group members.

Interaction Diagram

An interaction diagram shows the diversity of participation and the amount for each person. Two five-minute samples during an hour's meeting usually provide a reasonably accurate picture of interaction, and can be corrected and generalized from after the meeting with the less precise observations made during the rest of the meeting.

An easy form for showing interactions is illustrated in Figure 12. The arrow shows the person to whom the remarks were directed, or, if they are addressed to the total group, the arrow stops in the middle.

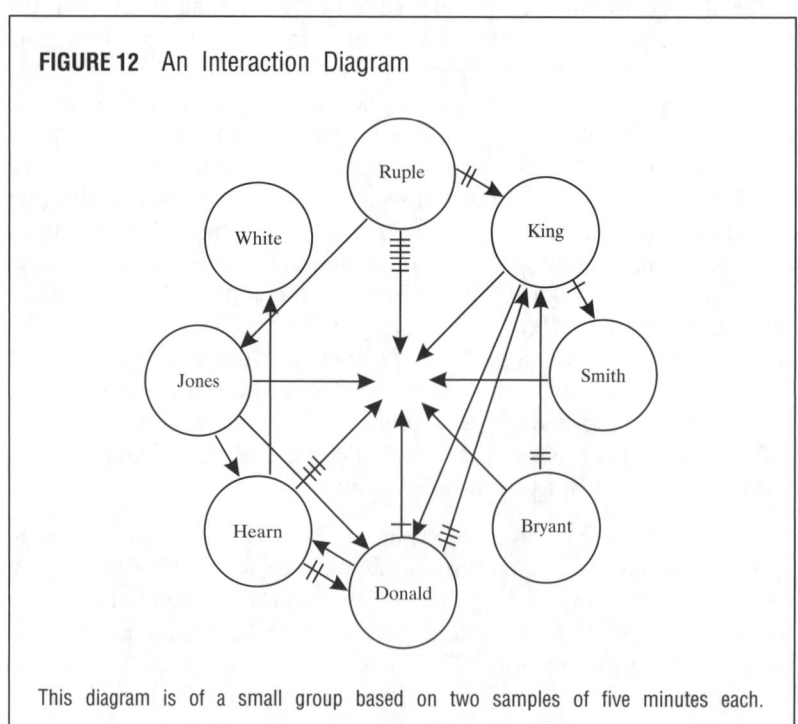

FIGURE 12 An Interaction Diagram

This diagram is of a small group based on two samples of five minutes each.

The number of times a person talked is tabulated by counting the number of arrows she sends out, plus the number of dash marks on each of the arrows. In Figure 12, King spoke 12 times and White did not participate. During this part of the meeting, the observer did not participate.

Appropriate group procedures are needed to facilitate decision making. The topics under the structure and effect of the chairperson's role in the guide suggest observation of the factors often directly related to the inefficient and frustrating problem-solving procedures of a group.

Survey of Group Development

The tool "Survey of Group Development" was designed for intermittent use with a group. The observer or staff person would ordinarily complete this form (seen on pages 82–84) after every few meetings and use it to chart the development of the group in these key areas. The tool has been used extensively by group participants as an aide to assessing and analyzing their group's operation. It is particularly useful for program evaluations and comparisons of programs in project teams, social service, rehabilitation, recreation, and informal educational programs. While the survey requires only 13 ticks, the average completion time is about 20 minutes.

Experience has shown that this survey is best completed following a group meeting or program activity, but the 13 dimensions should be the focus for observations during the meeting. Some observers find it helpful to jot down the 13 areas on a three-by-five card and glance over them during the meeting as a reminder.

As observers become more familiar with the 13 dimensions and skilled in their observations related to them, they find the four choices for each area do not allow them to record their real assessments. At this point they should either modify the suggested descriptions by changing a word here and there, or write up their own summary under each of the headings shown on Figure 13, "Dimensions of Group Growth."

However, if the survey is to be used for measurement and comparison purposes, modifications of the descriptions are not appropriate and observers should go back to selecting the box that most nearly describes the group. Comparisons of these critical areas of a group's development over a period of time provide a rather accurate measurement of a group's growth, as well as an indicator of group health and usefulness

FIGURE 13 Dimensions of Group Growth

The following is a comprehensive set of dimensions on which a group can be evaluated. The progress of the group in these 13 areas provides a summary of its health.

1. **Unity** (Degree of unity, cohesion, or "we-ness")
   - Is the group just a collection of individuals, or is there some common purpose and spirit based on friendships?

2. **Self-direction** (The group's own motive power)
   - Is the group apathetic, dominated by a single person, or self-propelled with all the members initiating?

3. **Group climate** (The extent to which members feel free to be themselves)
   - Are people inhibited and "uptight," or do they feel free to express their needs and desires within the framework of the total group's welfare?

4. **Distribution of leadership** (Extent to which leadership roles are distributed among members)
   - Does one member or a few members take leadership, or is leadership shared by all the members?

5. **Distribution of responsibility** (Extent to which responsibility is shared among members)
   - Do members tend to shirk responsibility, with one or two always carrying things out, or is responsibility distributed among all the members?

6. **Problem solving** (Group's ability to think straight, make use of everyone's ideas, and decide creatively about its problems)
   - Is decision making hasty or erratic, with confused movement toward decisions, or is there a good pooling of ideas, with an orderly pattern for decision making?

7. **Method of resolving disagreements with group** (How group works out disagreements)
   - Does one person arbitrarily resolve differences, is there a majority vote with the strongest sub-group dominating, or are there compromises and attempts to work out a consensus?

8. **Meets basic needs** (Extent to which group gives a sense of security, achievement, approval, recognition, and belonging)
   - Does the group experience add a little or a great deal to meeting the basic needs of all members?

9. **Variety of activities**
   - Are there dull routines with little variety of activity, or are different approaches tried that lead to considerable variety?

Continued next page

FIGURE 13 (continued)

10. **Depth of activities** (Extent to which activities are gone into in such a way that members can use full potentials, skills, and creativity)
    - Are the activities or discussions conducted in a superficial way, or is there real depth, with members being challenged to develop their abilities?

11. **Leader–member rapport** (Relations between the group and the designated leader)
    - Is the group indifferent toward the leader, is there hero worship of this person, or is there acceptance as a person and an integration into the group?

12. **Role of the leader** (Extent to which the group is centred around the designated leader)
    - Does the group revolve around the interests and personality of the leader, or do the members "carry the ball" themselves?

13. **Stability**
    - Is there a high absenteeism and turnover, or is the group stable in terms of the conditions under which it operates?

---

for program evaluation. It may seem that this survey is subject to observer judgment or bias, yet our research has shown that independent observers have a high inter-observer reliability (significant at .05 level) and that ratings by members, leaders, and supervisors correlate at the same high level of significance.

Roles of Group Members Guide

Seen on pages 80–81 this is one of the most popular observation tools as it encourages descriptions of individual behaviour and makes for specific feedback to each member. Leadership training groups find practising different roles and getting feedback on the practice very useful in developing a larger repertoire of roles, and in gaining skill and comfort in when to use them. Groups trying to increase their effectiveness will have the observer focus on the total group (not identifying individual roles), and perhaps show a frequency chart to illustrate the overplayed roles and the ones rarely taken, which the group might want to work at adding (see Viewpoint II — Member Roles, p. 9).

To make a complete record of a meeting using this guide is a full-time job and removes the observer from participating. To be a participant-observer, time samples can be used for intensive recording. A five-minute sample every 15 or 20 minutes works out pretty well. It is best if the time samples are determined ahead of time to increase the likelihood of their being a cross-section of the total meeting. Observing with roles of group members complements video recording of a group as both forms of observation make for specific feedback to individuals. This activity is particularly useful for training purposes where the goal is personal learning and skill development for individual members, such as group dynamics classes, leadership and management training, and personal growth groups.

Let us now look at a couple of technical problems that come up in using this observation guide. More than one role is often taken as a participant speaks, and it is difficult to decide how to categorize the input. A person may start off seeming to agree and build on a previous speaker's idea but ends up making a new proposal. Is this to be categorized as "supporting-encouraging" or "gives opinions"? While it is possible to list this contribution under both categories, the rule of thumb is to list it under the chief message it left with the group. In this case it would be "gives opinions" because a new proposal has more impact than some general agreement: "I am in general agreement with Noela's proposal, which I think this group has the resources to implement, yet I wonder if we might not do better having our own presentation and display two or three weeks later" (gives opinions). Or a question may be followed with a new proposal: "Why do some members want to have us attend city council and propose that they assist us with some special funding? Wouldn't we be better off with a major story in the newspaper or on local television?" (gives opinions). If in doubt, the observer could list them under both categories, and in the long run the group profile of roles would look pretty much the same.

It is more difficult to categorize an intervention when the true meaning is given a verbal camouflage, especially if it is a fairly long speech. While the content of the intervention should be taken at face value and categorized accordingly, the rule of thumb is that, when in doubt, either list it as giving opinions or just omit it from the record. Often, the tendency for a new observer is to puzzle over the intervention for a bit, and by then the next speaker may say something that influences the rating. For example, if Tom rambles on and it is not clear whether he is supporting a previous idea, giving information about it, or seeking others' opinions about it, and the next speaker says, "Yes, I, too, agree that this would make sense and that we should do it," there may be an influence to categorize Tom as giving opinions (agreement) or supporting-encouraging. The rule of thumb here is to try not to be influenced by a following statement in categorizing the previous one.

All of the task- and group-building roles can be helping or hindering the group — appropriateness to the situation and timing are the keys. Giving opinions, for example, before the problem is clear to everyone may not be helpful; yet if doing so clarifies the problem for some members, it may help. But testing feasibility before the problem is clear to everyone would not be helpful. Generally, the individual roles are not likely to be helpful and in the early days of working with this guide, Hedley called them non-functional roles. However, he found this was not always the case as an "out-of-field" joke often broke the tension, and a "digression" might end up having some value at a later point of time. And a "digression" for the observer might be an important contribution for several members.

Behaviour Frequency Observation Guide

The Behaviour Frequency Observation Guide (shown on page 75), like the Roles of Group Members Guide, is most useful in groups where indicators of the growth of individual members are needed, or in training, treatment, and personal development groups where feedback on individual behaviour is appropriate. Consequently, this format has been used extensively in alternative educational programs for youth, camp groups, classrooms, growth groups, and in leadership and management training. Typically, two or three members volunteer to complete the observation guide, or it may be used by the staff person and outside observer in a program evaluation project. The specific observational areas described in the guide may be revised to focus on the actual goals and objectives of the groups under study. This guide is most useful when it is completed by more than one observer over a length of time in which several ratings have been made.

A shorter version of the narrative record idea is the Survey of Group Activity form (shown on page 85), which is particularly useful for groups that meet once a week or for groups undergoing some constant evaluation process, such as treatment or therapy. It is also useful as a supervisory tool when the designated leader is in training and the group experience is part of that training (group leader trainee, student teacher or nurse, graduate student or program intern).

OTHER OBSERVATION AREAS

A number of other observation areas are listed in Figure 14, which the interested observer may want to use in cafeteria style, picking out additional categories to look at or starting from scratch to build his own observation guide. The items are in no particular order and are in addition to the areas mentioned in the previous guide sheets, though there is some overlapping.

Always included in any list of observation areas are the two major motivators that are likely to be in play:

• Control/power

• Self-advancement (recognition, status, promotion, monetary rewards

GROUP RECORDS

Group workers, teachers, and team leaders keep records of the growth of their groups in order to help the group grow and use the full potential of its members. As the workers make their observations of their groups and jot them down, aided by the observation guides presented in this book, they start to develop a longitudinal picture of the growth of the groups and their present status. This picture may be supplemented with additional data from the other methods described in *Assessing Group Dynamics* (Dimock & Devine, 1997; see also *Outcome-based Program Development and Evaluation* [Dimock, 2004]). These group records form the basis for the analysis of the group's strengths and weaknesses and the designated leaders' attempts to optimize their coaching roles. They also form the basis for any kind of systematic or planned group development. They may be used to measure the results of the group experience for the group's members, provide information for annual reports and interpretive statements of the agency, and to help to orient a new worker to the group in the future.

Group records provide a basis for supervision that is focused on helping the worker understand the group and improve its effectiveness in achieving the organization's goals. The major records for the worker to keep include Survey of Group Development (the major dimensions of group growth), Behaviour Frequency Observation Guide (major value dimensions of individual growth), and Survey of Member Activity. These three are supplemented by the more extensive group observation records described here and by the sociometric measures, member and

FIGURE 14 Cafeteria-Style Observation Categories

- *Group rules* (standards) — procedures for handing routines, dealing with absences, lateness, poor completion of jobs assigned, etc.
- Clarity of members in expressing ideas.
- How the designated leader handles group problems.
- Whether the designated leader shows favouritism among members.
- List the members according to their status in the group.
- How sensitive the designated leader is to the needs and interests of the members.
- Method of control used by group.
- Methods of resolving differences used by group.
- Non-verbal communication — gestures (nodding head, tapping fingers), facial expressions (bored, surprised, disgusted), posture, and position in relation to group.
- Seating arrangement — who sits next to whom, who sits or participates on the fringe of the group, who is always centrally located, who often leaves group.
- Who talks after whom (a great way to spot pairing and competition).
- Critical incidents during activity.
- Tension release through exuberant laughter or horseplay.
- List position of members on controversial topic and identify sub-groups and pairing.
- How well the program was planned.
- Use of available resources outside group (agency, community).
- Leadership style of designated leader (directing, coaching, facilitating, delegating).
- Respect and regard for facilities and equipment.
- Hidden agenda.
- Invisible committees.
- Pressures for and against making a decision.
- Stressing of pride in the group.
- Setting clear, challenging, and attainable goals.
- Arranging goals and work methods so that the group succeeds.
- Helping each member to be aware of his/her contribution to group success.
- Sex roles and stereotypes (male, female, androgynous).

parent ratings, interest finders, member reactions, and other personal data described in *Assessing Group Dynamics*.

Two other forms of records are worth mentioning: anecdotal records and narrative descriptions. These methods have traditionally been popular with nurses, teachers, and therapists.

Anecdotal Records

Essentially, an anecdotal record describes, in purely objective terms, an interesting or unusual event that happened either to an individual, a sub-group, or to the total group. Areas to consider for the possible writing of anecdotes have been described under observation headings; the major difference is the method of recording.

The job of the recorder is to select incidents worth reporting and describe them objectively. These incidents should describe a wide range of behaviour, both positive and negative, of individuals in the group and of total group dynamics. Single incidents do not have much meaning but as the anecdotes accumulate, they have real value as they present an over-a-period-of-time, objective set of descriptions that can be used for diagnostic and comparative purposes.

One of the best things about anecdotal records is that as they are brief descriptions of something that happened, people who were not part of the group can read them and make independent judgments about what was going on. These outside "judges" may be classmates, other organization staff, or supervisors, and their role is to help the observer check out possible bias by giving an independent summary or analysis of what they think is going on in the group. This approach is part of the triangulation method of increasing the accuracy of observation information by trying to get three different views of an event or group characteristic. Procedures for using judges' ratings of anecdotal records for measurement and program evaluation are described in the *Simplified Guide to Program Evaluation* book in this series.

Anecdotes should be dated to establish their sequence in time, and the setting or activity of the group should be mentioned to put the description in context. Identifying the noise, lack of concentration, and silly antics of a group come into perspective only if the observer records that it was the evening of the last day of school for the year. Each anecdote should be reported in a factual, objective way. Value judgment or interpretations by the recorder are best omitted unless they are necessary to make the picture clear.

Examples of Useful Anecdotes

- The class of nursing students (18 female and 3 male) were deciding how they would divide up into the assigned three project groups for their wellness assignment. Jean wanted to divide into groups by drawing names out of a hat. The others pooh-poohed this idea. Jean didn't say anything for the next 10 minutes and then left the room. The others paid no attention and continued their problem solving.

- As the group came back from the ballfield after losing the game, the boys became more and more quiet. Finally, after a period of silence, Hank said, "We should have won the damn game anyway." Tears streaked down his cheek. George and Tim wept a little, too.

- The 11 members of the board sat around in low chairs and each member had a thick folder of papers in front of him. After opening the meeting, Libby (chair) asked members to get out the consultant's report on revitalizing the organization.

Narrative/Descriptive Records

Narrative or descriptive records are kept in diary form with the worker describing what happened and how she felt and reacted to these happenings. These records are usually written shortly after the time span to be reported on has elapsed (a meeting or a day in a residential setting). Figure 15 on page 72, "Types of Descriptions a Narrative Record Should Contain," will be helpful here. Added to this is the basic information about the group, names of those present, time and place of meeting, setting of meeting, and other conditions affecting the meeting (weather, holiday, exam period, etc.). The focus of the narrative record is on the group process — how members reacted to one another and to the designated leader — and not as much on the program content. The major weakness of narrative records is the time involved in writing them up, but this can be considerably reduced by tape-recording the narrative description (small cassette or electronic recorders are best), and having a typist type up the records later. The other problem with narrative and anecdotal records is the difficulty most people have writing non-judgmental descriptions. Learning to do it represents a considerable investment of time (graduate students rarely learn it in a 13-week course), and it is likely only worthwhile for those planning to use the methods extensively.

Records are an accepted part of systematic group work and of educational supervision, but the question raised by many students and

---

FIGURE 15 Types of Descriptions a Narrative Record Should
Contain

1. A description of the setting, who was present, and what the group did.
   (a) A description of activities (*what* the group did).
   (b) A description of feelings and emotions around the activities (*how* they
       did it).
   (c) A description of how the activities came into being (member planning
       session, spontaneous, organization assignment, etc.).

2. A description of the group's planning process. (This should tell not just what
   was discussed, but how the group planned and how decisions were reached.)

3. A description of how the members functioned as a group.
   (a) Degree of cohesiveness (unity vs. cliques, conflicts, and individual
       behaviour).
   (b) Distribution of task-responsibility roles (few, some, or all) and how
       these roles were decided on (take turns, volunteer, appoint, etc.).

4. A description of individual members in the group.
   (a) Group adjustment.
       i. Analysis of acceptance by group.
       ii. Typical roles in group interaction (leadership, responsibility, non-func-
           tional behaviour, individual roles).
       iii. Typical roles in group planning.
   (b) Participant learning or skill development (these may be technical skills—
       learn to make copper ashtray) or human relations skills (learn to accept
       wise remarks from others).
   (c) Individual behaviour.

5. Role of designated leader in group life. Description of:
   (a) Areas of direction and control.
   (b) Areas of limit setting and endorsing.
   (c) Areas of stimulating and suggesting.
   (d) Areas of showing technical know-how (how to write an accident report
       or use a technique).
   (e) Areas of facilitating (helping things to come about).
   (f) Use of relationships to influence individual behaviour (modelling).

6. Relation of group to other groups, the organization, or the community.

---

beginning workers is, "What records should I keep?" The most honest
answer is "those records that will help you to work with the group
more effectively in order that it can achieve its objectives and the
organization's goals." There is no general answer as the background
and training of the worker and the unique aspects of the group make a

great deal of difference. Volunteer workers with little professional background will want simple, straightforward records that will gradually increase their understanding. Advanced professional workers doing intensive work and trying to improve their practice or those doing research will want complete records, combining most of the material described in these two sections. Be encouraged to make your own choices.

Hedley's choice has been to encourage workers in the many different organizations where he has worked or been a consultant to use three surveys (Survey of Group Development, either of the individual surveys — Roles of Group Members or Behaviour Frequency Observation Guide, and Survey of Member Activity) as the basic records and to supplement these with other information, especially friendship finders or social relations indexes, as the situation appears to warrant it. In settings where there is a major emphasis on educational supervision, the narrative record is very useful for the worker's growth, as it allows the worker to describe things in his own words, and is more flexible than check-off sheets. Our rule continues to be to not collect more data than we can use, but to try to expand our resources and develop our skills wherever possible.

REPORTING OBSERVATIONS TO YOUR GROUP

There is a great challenge in reporting observations to your group in your role as a *process-observer* or designated observer that has more to do with the way you present your material than with the quality of your material. Groups like to feel that their observer, or anyone helping to process group experiences, is working on an assignment by the group and is responsible to the group for that task. It is a service role much like the group recorder, who makes a report on the content of the group's meetings and looks for additions and corrections. The excitement of the observer role and the opportunity to watch individual roles and overall group operation makes it easy to move to a judgmental or evaluative stance in reporting group observations. This tends to distance the observer from the group by setting her up as an evaluator who tells the group, and individuals, what has been going wrong. The group may react by rejecting the observer's report actively — that is, arguing against it. Or the group may reject it passively by politely thanking the observer and than quickly going on to the next item of business. After two or three such experiences the group finds it "doesn't have time" for the observer's report, and looking at the group's process becomes a low priority and gradually disappears as a group activity.

Groups that have continuing success with an observer function usually share it around the group with each member taking turns to report, usually for one to four group meetings. In an effort to move the observer's report from a lecture on what the group did that was helpful and not helpful, many groups either assign two observers or expect everyone to be a *participant-observer* and turn the observer report into a group discussion, with many participants sharing their perceptions of what happened at the meeting and how it felt for them. As mentioned earlier, when Hedley is the *designated observer* or the *program-observer* (research-observer), he enlists a group member to join him in the observer role as this helps to get a member perspective on group process. It also encourages other members to participate in the discussion of the observers' report.

As an observer, it is helpful to make a few provocative observations of key areas of the group's process in a descriptive rather than interpretive or judgmental fashion. Think of yourself as announcing a hockey game on radio, sports announcer-style — that is, describing as accurately as possible the key plays in the game with enough animation to keep all your listeners on the edge of their seats. Too much data, even if it is accurate and of high quality, is boring and counter-productive. Your goal is to present a crisp yet comprehensive report that is tantalizing and will provoke members to respond in a general discussion. Figure 16 suggests how this might be done.

This provocative stage is furthered if you present your observations in a descriptive way and then raise a number of questions about them. If you are prone to making interpretations, try to make two or three possible interpretations of the same event so that others can join in trying to figure out what is happening, and why. Or try to pose your interpretations as hunches or questions — "Estelle was very emotional in her participation today, and I wonder if that was related to what was going on in the group, or to something outside the group." "Irene made a number of interventions today that tried to keep us on track and accomplishing our tasks of recruiting new members. I'm not sure if this was an important task for her, or if she just wanted to complete it as quickly as possible." "Dick, Bob, and Sylvia raised a number of issues today about the use of our Planned Programming Budget System, but I wasn't sure if they were meant to help us use the process more effectively or if they were designed to question our continued use of the PPBS approach."

FIGURE 16 Observer Report Example

Content Observation (factual report)	Progress Observation (non-judgmental description)	Process Comment (observer's hunches)	Results of Observations and Process Comment
The group made a number of suggestions for revisions to the vacation plan. None of them gained very much acceptance.	All of the suggested revisions came from senior staff. Junior staff did not participate in discussion (many appeared bored).	"It seems all the suggestions and discussion came from senior staff. I wonder why none of the newer staff contributed to the discussion?"	Most of the newer people felt it was not their place to discuss vacation schedules. They felt that to do so would appear presumptuous to senior staff. When these feelings were made clear the discussion proceeded with input from the junior staff.
The proposed plan and schedule for dealing with next year's budget was discussed for 50 minutes. No decision was made about it.	Four times the group went through the same cycle of reviewing the proposal's strengths and weaknesses with no new data emerging.	"I'm wondering if the group finds the proposal unacceptable or is·just trying to avoid the whole budget issue or really wants to deal with the proposal for the experimental program first?"	The group agreed that they were avoiding the budget issue because of the difficulty of the needed cutbacks. They agreed to first clear the deck of the experimental program proposal and then really buckle down and start with the budget issues.

"The group seemed to be very lighthearted tonight and I don't know if it was related to the difficulty of the task, or just a reflection that this is our first board meeting in a while when we haven't had a very heavy agenda." The role of the observer is to provide data that the group can use to increase its effectiveness, and the more the group can identify with the data and get excited by it, the more likely it is to be used in group planning.

Another approach that generates group interest is to raise the question at the close of the report as to where this observation report seems to fit into a theory of group development. If the group is familiar with the Roles of Group Members (Viewpoint II, p. 9) theory, they might discuss the relation of *Task* and *Group Building* roles or comment on the increase in *Non-functional* activity. If the group knows the Interpersonal Relations theory (Viewpoint III, p. 12) they might want to review members' comfort and security with their acceptance and position in the group in light of the observer's report. These discussions about the developmental status of the group often lead to agreements about activities and behaviours that will help increase members' satisfaction with the group and make it more effective.

SUMMARY COMMENTS

Your authors believe that observing groups can be a lot of fun as so many of life's experiences then take on a new and more interesting reality. We will occasionally observe another table group in a restaurant and guess what kind of a group it is (friends, family, work colleagues, or a bridge, church, or society group) and why they are there. Then, usually, Hedley goes and asks them. Often he has been invited to sit and chat, have a drink or dessert with them, etc. Our goal with this book has been to broaden the kinds of things you observe and to give them more meaning. We expect the ways of looking at groups and the explanations of usual group dynamics have helped you understand your observations and given them a useful perspective. But we strongly believe in learning by doing.

We give great importance to the value of the learning that group observers accumulate from their own experiences. Any leaders who can systematically observe a few groups will have their own natural demonstrations to study. If they keep some records and try to understand the process of the group, noting similarities and differences among them, they can amass a storehouse of understandings that books can seldom provide. These experience-based learnings can be the foundation for efforts to make their groups more successful and effective.

Observation Tools

Behaviour Frequency Observation Guide

Group _____ Date _____ Observer _____

Rate the frequency of each person's behaviour using:

0 = not observed

1 = once or twice

2 = a few times

3 = frequently

Name

1. Initiated activities

2. Assumed leadership in group

3. Made friendly approaches to others

4. Withdrawn or out of group

5. Got angry and shouted or sulked

6. Showed vim and enthusiasm for activity

7. Showed off, boasted, sought attention

8. Disrupted or disturbed group

9. Fidgeted, twitched, appeared nervous

10. Helped others to participate or learn

11. Helped group to evaluate its performance

12. Praised or supported others

Group Observation Guide

Group _____   Date _____

Time _____ to _____   Observer _____

CLIMATE

(*Physical*) distractions, ventilation, lighting, seating arrangements conducive to interaction?

(*Emotional*) formal — informal? accepting — judgmental? cooperative — competitive? supportive? friendly? enthusiastic?

- Do members express feelings (fears, desires, concerns)?

INVOLVEMENT

- Why are members here? absenteeism — lateness?
- Stake in present problem or activity? Commitment to group?
- Attentive? (List who) Restless? Withdrawn?
- Individual issues — literacy/language, hearing, physical, cognitive.

INTERACTION

- Lines of communication (1 to 1, 1 to group, or all through leader)?
- Distribution of participation (what % of the group did half the talking)? Overparticipators? Underparticipators?
- Who has the power in the group? Sub-groups or cliques?
- Impact of group size on interaction?
- Balance of task and group-building roles?
  - _____ % Task
  - _____ % Group
- Are people listening and building on the ideas of others?
- Non-verbal behaviour? gestures — facial expression — posture?

COHESION

- Degree of group solidarity? Group vs. individual interests?
- Group norms observed? Who doesn't conform? Strength of pressures to conform? Readiness to accept majority decisions?
- How well does group work as a team?

PRODUCTIVITY

- Clarity of goals? realistic — understood? percent supporting goals?
- Did members contribute to statement of goals?
- Was there a flexible plan for reaching goal? Understood by all? Followed?
- Effectiveness of procedures and outcomes evaluated regularly?
- What steps did group use in making decisions? Where did it get off-track?
- Were decisions from last session carried out? Started and stopped on time?
- Was next session planned for? How?
- Effect of leader/chairperson, chief executive, recorder/secretary roles?
- Style of leadership? Impact on participation? Percent of content and process?
- Notes on productivity (content tags)

Roles of Group Members — Definition Sheet

TASK ROLES

1. **Defines problems** — group problem is defined: overall purpose of group is outlined.

2. **Seeks information** — requests factual information about group problem or methods of procedure, or for clarification of suggestions.

3. **Gives information** — offers facts or general information about group problem, methods to be used, or clarifies a suggestion.

4. **Seeks opinions** — asks for the opinions of others relevant to discussion.

5. **Gives opinions** — states beliefs or opinions relevant to discussion.

6. **Tests feasibility** — questions reality, checks practicality of suggested solutions.

GROUP-BUILDING AND MAINTENANCE ROLES

7. **Coordinating** — a recent statement is clarified and related to another statement in such a way as to bring them together. Proposed alternatives are reviewed for the group.

8. **Mediating-harmonizing** — interceding in disputes or disagreements and attempting to reconcile them. Highlights similarities in views.

9. **Orienting-facilitating** — keeps group on track, points out deviations from agreed-upon procedures or from direction of group discussion. Helping group process along, proposing other structures or procedures to make group more effective.

10. **Supporting-encouraging** — expressing approval of another's suggestion, praising others' ideas, being warm and responsive to ideas of others.

11. **Following** — going along with the movement of the group, accepting ideas of others, expressing agreement.

INDIVIDUAL ROLES

12. **Blocking** — interfering with the progress of the group by arguing, resisting, and disagreeing beyond reason. Or by coming back to same "dead" issue later. Taking up air time.

13. **Out of field** — withdrawing from discussion, daydreaming, doing something else, whispering to others, leaving room, etc.

14. **Digressing** — getting off the subject, leading discussion in some "personally oriented direction," or expanding a brief statement into a long, nebulous speech.

Roles of Group Members

Group _____ Date _____ Observer _____

Put initials of each member at top of each column.

TASK ROLES

- Defines problem
- Seeks information
- Gives information
- Seeks opinions
- Gives opinions
- Tests feasibility

GROUP-BUILDING AND MAINTENANCE ROLE

- Coordinating
- Mediating-Harmonizing
- Orienting-Facilitating
- Supporting-Encouraging
- Following

INDIVIDUAL ROLES

- Blocking
- Out of Field
- Digressing

If a general, rather than individual, picture of the group is desired, the first column can be used to show the total times that function was taken by any group member. This would then show what functions were being over-played and under-played in the group.

Survey of Group Development

Group _____   Date _____

Time _____ to _____   Observer _____

For each area, place an "X" in the box that most nearly describes the group.

1. UNITY (Degree of unity, cohesion, or "we-ness")

   ☐ Group is just a collection of individuals or sub-groups; little group feeling.

   ☐ Some group feeling. Unity stems more from external factors than from real friendship.

   ☐ Group is very close and there is little room or felt need for other contacts and experience.

   ☐ Strong common purpose and spirit based on real friendships. Group usually sticks together.

2. SELF-DIRECTION (The group's own motive power)

   ☐ Little drive from anywhere, either from members or designated leader.

   ☐ Group has some self-propulsion but needs considerable push from designated leader.

   ☐ Domination from a strong single member, a clique, or the designated leader.

   ☐ Initiation, planning, executing, and evaluating comes from total group.

3. GROUP CLIMATE (The extent to which members feel free to be themselves)

   ☐ Climate inhibits good fun, behaviour, and expression of desire, fears and opinions.

   ☐ Members express themselves but without observing interests of total group.

   ☐ Members freely express needs and desires; joke, tease, and argue to detriment of the group.

   ☐ Members feel free to express themselves but limit expression to total group welfare.

4. DISTRIBUTION OF LEADERSHIP (Extent to which leadership roles are distributed among members)

   ☐ A few members always take leadership roles. The rest are passive.

   ☐ Some of the members take leadership roles but many remain passive followers.

   ☐ Many members take leadership but one or two are continually followers.

   ☐ Leadership is shared by all members of the group.

Continued next page

5. DISTRIBUTION OF RESPONSIBILITY (Extent to which responsibility is shared among members)

☐ Everyone tries to get out of jobs.

☐ Responsibility carried by a few members.

☐ Many members accept responsibilities but do not carry them out.

☐ Responsibilities are distributed among and carried out by nearly all members.

6. PROBLEM SOLVING (Group's ability to think straight, make use of everyone's ideas, and decide creatively about its problems)

☐ Not much thinking as a group. Decisions made hastily, or group lets leader or worker do most of the thinking.

☐ Some cooperative thinking but group gets tangled up in pet ideas of a few. Confused movement toward solutions.

☐ Some thinking as a group but not yet an orderly process.

☐ Good pooling of ideas and orderly thought. Everyone's ideas are used to reach final plan.

7. METHOD OF RESOLVING DISAGREEMENTS WITH GROUP (How group works out disagreements)

☐ Group waits for the designated leader to resolve disagreements.

☐ Strongest sub-group dominates through a vote and majority rule.

☐ Compromises are effected by each sub-group giving up something.

☐ Group as a whole arrives at a solution that satisfies all members and that is better than any single suggestion.

8. MEETS BASIC NEEDS (Extent to which group gives a sense of security, achievement, approval, recognition, and belonging)

☐ Group experience adds little to the meeting of most members' needs.

☐ Group experience contributes to some degree to basic needs of most members.

☐ Group experience contributes substantially to basic needs of most members.

☐ Group contributes substantially to basic needs of all members.

Continued next page

9. VARIETY OF ACTIVITIES

☐ Little variety in activities — stick to same things.

☐ Some variety in activities.

☐ Considerable variety in activities. Try out new activities.

☐ Great variety in activities. Continually trying out new ones.

10. DEPTH OF ACTIVITIES (Extent to which activities are gone into in such a way that members can use full potentials, skills, and creativity)

☐ Little depth in activities — just scratching the surface.

☐ Some depth but members are not increasing their skills.

☐ Considerable depth in activities. Members able to utilize some of their abilities.

☐ Great depth in activities. Members find each a challenge to develop their abilities.

11. LEADER–MEMBER RAPPORT (Relations between the group and the designated leader)

☐ Antagonistic or resentful.

☐ Indifferent toward leader. Friendship neither sought nor rejected. Non-communicative.

☐ Friendly and interested. Attentive to leader's suggestions.

☐ Intimate relations: openness and sharing. Strong rapport.

12. ROLE OF THE LEADER (Extent to which the group is centred around the designated leader)

☐ Activities, discussion, and decisions revolve around interests, desires, and needs of leader.

☐ Group looks to leader for suggestions and ideas. Leader decides when member gets in a jam.

☐ Leader acts as stimulator — suggests ideas or other ways of doing things. Helps group find ways of making own decisions.

☐ Leader stays out of discussion and makes few suggestions of things to do. Lets members carry the ball themselves.

13. STABILITY

☐ High absenteeism and turnover; influences group a great deal.

☐ High absenteeism and turnover; little influence on group growth.

☐ Some absenteeism and turnover with minor influence on group.

☐ Low absenteeism rate and turnover. Group very stable.

Survey of Group Activity

Group _____ Date _____ Observer _____

1. Briefly describe what the group did and accomplished.

    _____

    _____

2. General reaction of the group and individuals to these activities.

    _____

    _____

3. How did the group plan? How were decisions made or activities decided on?

    _____

    _____

4. Description of group relationships (sub-grouping or pairing, dependency, conflict, power plays, use of group pressure, group building).

    _____

    _____

5. Description of individual's behaviour (cooperative, out of field, seeking attention — anything unusual or a problem).

    _____

    _____

Bibliography

Anderson, J. (1985). Working with groups: Little known facts that challenge well known myths. *Small Group Behaviour*, 16 (3), 257–283.

Bennis, Warren G. (1964). "Patterns and vicissitudes in T-group development" in *T.-Group Theory and Laboratory Method* eds. L.P. Bradford, J.R. Gibb and K.D. Benne, pp. 248–278. New York: Wiley.

Bem Sandra L. (1975). Sex-role adaptability: One consequence of psychological androgyny. *Journal of Personality & Social Psychology* 31, 634–643.

———. (1977). "Bem Sex-role Inventory (BSRI)" in *The 1977 Annual Handbook for Group Facilitators* eds. J. Jones and J.W. Pfeiffer, pp. 83–87. San Diego, CA: University Associates.

———. (1978). *Bem Sex-role Inventory*. Palo Alto, CA: Consulting Psychologists Press.

Bion, W.R. (1961). *Experiences in Groups*. New York: Basic Books.

Dimock, Hedley G. (1987). *Groups: Leadership and Group Development*. San Diego, C.A.: University Associates.

———. (1992). *Intervention and Empowerment: Helping Organizations to Change*. North York, Ont.: Captus Press.

———. (1993). *Intervention and Collaboration: Helping Organizations to Change*. San Diego, CA: Pfeiffer & Co.

———. (1997). *A Simplified Guide to Program Evaluation*. Rev'd ed. North York, Ont.: Captus Press.

———. (2004). *Outcome-Based Program Evaluation*. Rev'd ed. North York, Ont.: Captus Press.

Dimock, Hedley G., & Devine, Irene. (1994). *Making Workgroups Effective*. North York, Ont.: Captus Press.

———. (1995). *Training for Planned Change*, 3d ed. North York, Ont.: Captus Press

———. (1996). *Managing Dynamic Groups*, 3d ed. North York, Ont.: Captus Press.

———. (1997). *Assessing Group Dynamics*, 3d ed. North York, Ont.: Captus Press.

Gibb, Jack R. (1978). *Trust: A New Theory of Personal and Organizational Development*. Los Angeles: Guild of Tudors Press.

Hare, A. Paul. (1976). *Handbook of Small Group Research*, 2nd ed. New York: Free Press.

Heyens, R. and Lippitt, R. (1954). "Systematic observational techniques" in *Handbook of Social Psychology* ed. G. Lindzey, pp. 370–404. Reading, Mass.: Addison-Wesley.

Heyens, R., & Zander, A. (1953). "Observation of group behaviour" in *Research Methods in the Behavioral Sciences* eds. L. Festinger and D. Katz, pp. 381–417. New York: Dryden.

Hill, W.F., & Gruner, L. (1973). A study of development in open and closed groups. *Small Group Behaviour*, 4, 355–381.

Kass, R. (2005) *Theories of Small Group Development*, 3rd Rev'd ed. Montreal: Centre for Human Relations and Community Studies, Concordia University.

Kass, R. (1983). *The Apology Stance in the Learning Process*. Unpublished doctoral dissertation, University of Toronto.

Kormanski, Charles L. (1985). "A Situational Leadership® approach to groups using the Tuckman model of group development" in *The 1985 Annual: Developing Human Resources* eds. L.D. Goodstein and J.W. Pfeiffer, pp. 217–225. San Diego, CA: University Associates.

Kuypers, B.C., Davies D., & Glaser, K.H. (1986). Developmental arrestation in self-analytic groups. *Small Group Behaviour*, 17 (3), 269–302.

Lacoursiere, R. (1982). A group method in clinical legal education. *Canadian Journal of Psychiatry*, 27 (3), 253–254.

Lacoursiere, R. (1980). *The life cycle of groups: Group developmental stage theory*. New York: Human Sciences Press.

Lacoursiere, R. (1974). A group method to facilitate learning during the stages of a psychiatric affiliation. *International Journal of Group Psychotherapy*, 24, 342–351.

Lewin, K. (1951). *Field Theory in Social Science: Selected Theoretical Papers*. New York, NY: Harper & Row.

Miles, Matthew B. (1981). *Learning to Work in Group*, 2nd ed. New York: Teachers College.

Napier, Rodney, & Gershenfeld, Matti. (1981). *Groups: Theory and Experience*, 2nd ed. Boston: Houghton-Mifflin.

Panel on Accountability and Governance in the Voluntary Sector. (1999). *Building on Strengths: Improving Governance and Accountability in Canada's Voluntary Sector* (Ottawa: Secretariat Panel on Accountability and Governance in the Voluntary Sector). Also available on-line: http://www.vsr-trsb.net/pagvs/Book.pdf.

Pattern, Michael Q. (1980). *Qualitative Evaluation Methods*. Beverly Hills, CA: Sage.

Pfeiffer, J. William. (1991). *Theories and Models in Applied Behavioral Science*, Volume II — Groups. San Diego, CA: Pfeiffer & Co.

Schutz, William C. (1958). *FIRO — A Three Dimensional Theory of Interpersonal Behaviour*. New York: Rinehart & Co., Inc. [Reprinted as *The Interper-*

sonal Underworld. Palo Alto, CA: Science and Behaviour Books, 1966; and Mill Valley, CA: Will Schutz Associates, 1989.]

Shaw, Marvin E. (1981). *Group Dynamics*, 3rd ed. New York: McGraw-Hill.

Stock, D., & Thelen, H. (1958). *Emotional Dynamics and Group Culture: Experimental Studies of Individual and Group Behavior.* Washington, D.C.: National Training Laboratories.

Tuckman, B.W., & Jensen, M.A.C. (1977). "Stages of small group development revisited," *Group and Organizational Studies* 2 (4), 419–427.

Zander, Alvin. (1982). *Making Groups Effective*. San Francisco: Jossey-Bass.
———. (1951). "Systematic observation of small face-to-face groups" in *Research Methods in Social Relations* by M. Jahoda, M. Deutsch & S.W. Cook, 516–538. New York: Dryden.